"I Am Looking to the North for My Life"

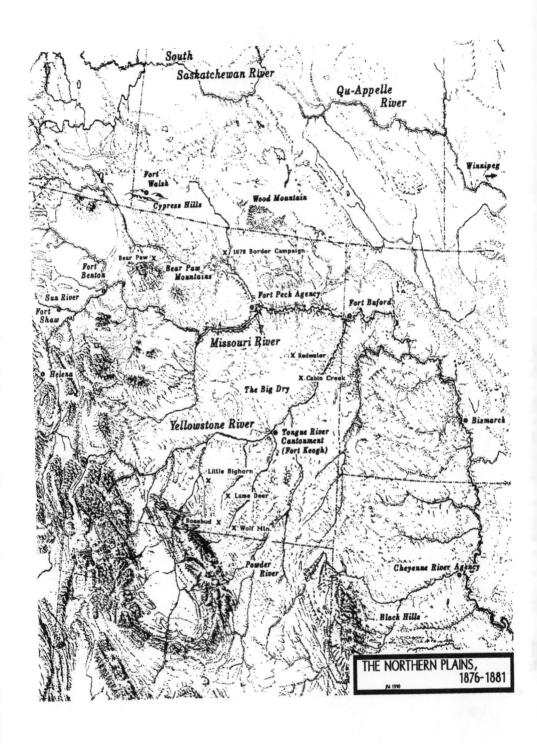

THE NORTHERN PLAINS,
1876-1881

"I Am Looking to the North for My Life"

Sitting Bull, 1876–1881

Joseph Manzione

University of Utah Press
Salt Lake City

Volume 25 of the University of Utah Publications
in the American West
Copyright © 1991 University of Utah Press
All rights reserved
Second printing 1991

LIBRARY OF CONGRESS CATALOGING-IN-PUBLICATION DATA
Manzione, Joseph A., 1957–
  "I am looking to the North for my life"—Sitting Bull, 1876–1881/ Joseph
A. Manzione.
    p.   cm. — (University of Utah publications in the American
West ; v. 25)
  Includes bibliographical references (p.   ) and index.
  ISBN 0-87480-354-3 (hard : alk. paper)
  1. Sitting Bull, 1834?–1890. 2. Dakota Indians—Biography.
3. Dakota Indians—Government relations. 4. Dakota Indians—
Removal. I. Title. II. Series.
  E99.D1S6123 1990 1991
  978'.0497502—dc20
  [B]   90-52747
                                                                  CIP

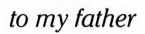

to my father

CONTENTS

PREFACE

Someone reading from among the many published accounts of the battle at the Little Bighorn may wonder what happened to the Sioux warriors who fought and then disappeared as soon as the dust had settled from the clear Montana air. The origins of the war for the Northern Plains in 1876 have already been described in detail; the steady encroachment of white civilization on the Black Hills is a good example of just what was wrong with United States–Native American affairs in the nineteenth century, and it has been cited often enough. The military operations in the Yellowstone River valley that summer have been subjected to successive waves of mythologizing and demythologizing for over a hundred years.

What did happen to the Sioux after the Little Bighorn? Cognizant of the climactic literary character of "Custer's Last Stand," many writers and historians have added, almost as a puzzled afterthought, that resistance seemed to melt away. More soldiers came, and the Indians gave up and trickled back onto the reservations in Dakota Territory. Some followed Sitting Bull into exile in Canada.

"Some followed Sitting Bull into exile in Canada" was a phrase that sparked my interest several years ago when I began this study. At the time it seemed to me that if the man many white Americans of the late nineteenth century regarded as the "perpetrator of the Custer massacre" had actually led some of his people into exile in a foreign country, the act would not be a postscript to a military campaign, but the beginning of a diplomatic event.

In that case, the options open to the American government were decidedly different from those accorded to U.S. military commanders chasing Kickapoo Indians across the Mexican border in 1873 or Apaches in the 1880s. It was one thing to send troops into the desolate regions beyond the Rio Grande, violating the sovereignty of a small, poor nation. It was quite another to go after a group of Indians given sanctuary by local authorities in the name of the government of Her Majesty, the Queen of England. The realities of the international situation and the delicacy of relations between the United States and Great Britain during this period would dictate negotiation, not armed invasion, along the northern border with Canada.

The Sioux hegira to Canada never seriously threatened British-American relations. Far more important problems affected the interests of both nations during the years 1876–1881, although perhaps none quite matched the emotionally explosive potential of the Sioux exile. To the American public, the idea of "the savages" aligning with "Perfidious Albion" brought together two extremely negative images. But the issue did not develop into anything more than a serious irritant that demonstrated the narrow range of acceptable diplomatic behavior between two often antagonistic nations.

There are other interesting facets to this issue. The story itself—a tragedy, the last days of the nonreservation Sioux, grimly struggling to hang on to their lives and culture—is compelling. Also, the drama brought together three fascinating historical characters from the post–Civil War frontier era: Sitting Bull, perhaps the most famous of Native American leaders; Col. Nelson A. Miles, a controversial soldier who was arguably the U.S. Army's best frontier field commander; and James M. Walsh, a competent, compassionate Canadian officer who exercised great influence over the early affairs of the North-West Mounted Police.

Finally, this episode offers opportunities to understand more about the often unique and sometimes similar experiences of the American and Canadian frontiers. I was particularly interested in comparing the methods that the U.S. Army and the North-West Mounted Police used to handle relations with the Sioux, and in comparing the attitudes of citizens on both sides of the border toward the Indians. When all of these elements are fit together, the hegira of the Sioux in Canada may transcend its narrow applications to general American or Canadian history and perhaps offer some instructive commentary on a number of issues in the late nineteenth century.

Mistakes in this book are, of course, my own. I owe acknowledgment and an expression of gratitude to a number of people. Robert Goldberg, Floyd O'Neill, and Sandra Taylor of the University of Utah all served on the thesis committee for which this project was initiated; their ideas and criticisms were much appreciated. Brigham D. Madsen, also of the University of Utah, was my committee chairman, and for his patience and encouragement I am deeply in debt. During my doctoral program at the University of Michigan, wide-ranging conversations and seminars with Bradford Perkins and John Shy in the areas of U.S. diplomatic history, British-American relations, and military history provided material for thought, and reinforced many of the weak areas in the manuscript. Finally, a special thanks to my spouse, Kate, who did as much as anyone could reasonably be expected to do.

INTRODUCTION

In the spring of 1876 the high, dry eastern plains of Montana Territory were virtually empty of settlement. A landscape of rolling prairie and low, rocky hills bisected by deep ravines, it held little interest for anyone beyond the occasional band of Plains Indians who found forage, wood, and water along its creeks. The region was not yet organized. To the east, in the Dakotas, the United States Army maintained a few forts. In the west the mining and trading towns of Helena, Deer Lodge, and Virginia City lay beneath the ramparts of the Rocky Mountains. Only the town of Fort Benton intruded upon the solitude of these plains, at the end of the steamboat run from Bismarck up the Missouri River, a primary route of transportation.

In the East, the nation was preparing for the centennial celebration, and participating in the political ritual of choosing a president. It appeared as if the Democrats might win. After eight tumultuous years of Grant administration scandals, many Americans were convinced that the Republican Party, the party of Lincoln and the Union, was rife with corruption. Others feared the prospect of a Democrat in the White House, especially during a time of reconstruction, industrialization, economic and social disruption, and increasing labor unrest. The political environment in the United States was volatile. Many believed that a suitable catalyst could ignite it.

The newspapers were filled with news of the coming elections, as well as local items and the latest reports from Europe. The possibility existed that Russia would declare war against the Ottoman Empire, and the Turks were trying to enlist Great Britain's aid in the ongoing struggle for advantage among the European powers. Britain was not popular in the United States. The heritage of the Revolution and the War of 1812 invoked an almost ritualistic hostility toward the Empire. Relations were further poisoned by the "British factor" in the Civil War; the Alabama case, a highly publicized attempt to mediate damage claims by the United States for the activities of Confederate raiders outfitted in Britain during the war, had convinced Americans of cynical motives behind British international policy. Political organizations, particularly in the Northeast, used this hostility to whip up support among Irish immigrants. Other groups agitated for annexation of the last British bastion in North America: the Dominion of Canada, especially the sparsely populated lands west of the Canadian Shield.

Another major news item was an "Indian War" on the Northern Plains. Gold had been discovered in the Black Hills and thousands of white miners and entrepreneurs flooded into the area. The Black Hills constituted a large and sacred section of the Great Sioux Reservation created eight years before, and the Indians resented the invasion. Many of the Sioux left the reservation for traditional hunting ranges in the unorganized lands of the Powder River and Yellowstone River valley, away from white interference.

Federal officials decided to use the army to flush them out and force them to return. Responsibility for this operation was divided between the Army Department of the Platte in the south, and the Department of the Dakota, a command encompassing the Northern Plains and Montana territory. Gen. Philip Sheridan, commander of the Platte, sent units into northern Wyoming under Gen. George Crook in the spring of 1876. At the same time, Alfred Terry, the commanding general of the Dakota, led another army group west up the Yellowstone River. Terry ordered a subordinate, Col. John Gibbon of the military District of Montana, to move a third group east from Fort Shaw on the Sun River. With Crook in the south, Terry in the north and east, and Gibbon converging from the west, Sheridan and General of the Army William T. Sherman hoped to trap the Sioux in the middle, forcing a decisive action. The operation was considered highly newsworthy: newspaper correspondents followed Crook's and Terry's commands, filing their reports for publication on front pages across the nation.

Several thousand Indians camped in the vicinity of the Little Bighorn River on the southeastern plains of Montana. Although the American public generally regarded the conflict as a struggle between civilization and a savage "Indian nation," the Sioux were actually a loose confederacy of many tribal elements, joined by associated groups of Northern Cheyenne and Arapaho. A great deal of interaction took place between these groups, and under the pressure and attrition of white expansion, the distinction between them sometimes blurred. Loyalties and the political structure of this confederacy differed substantially from white perceptions of a united and discrete people, with headmen from definable constituencies. The Sioux and their allies were more often an unpredictable association of culture and convenience. Unity depended upon circumstance, or the popularity of a particular cause or leader.

The cause of unity was particularly strong in the late spring and early summer of 1876. White encroachment upon the Black Hills and the military operations under Crook and Terry produced one of the largest concentrations of Native Americans in the Trans-Mississippi West in the nineteenth century. They banded together for self-defense. Among them were many who advocated a final stand to preserve what was left of their land and culture.

In June 1876 Terry sent Lt. Gen. George Armstrong Custer and his regiment up the Rosebud Creek from its mouth on the Yellowstone River to scout out the position of the Sioux. The Seventh Cavalry rode off to perhaps the most notorious military disaster in American history. The unit was decimated on the slopes above the Little Bighorn, while Crook's command was stopped by the Sioux near the headwaters of the Rosebud. The aftermath of these engagements would disrupt military operations in the West for months to come.

The news reached the East in time for the centennial celebration on July 4th. Demands for renewed war against the Sioux mingled with calls for a revision of Indian policy. But reforms soon stalled in Congress, victimized by the political climate and the influence of various conflicting economic, religious, and regional interests. The demise of the Sioux did not occur in the smoke and fury of a decisive battle, nor in a final surrender. Sioux resistance seemed to melt away, sorely puzzling American observers. At last only Sitting Bull remained at large, living in exile at Wood Mountain in the Northwest Territories of Canada with perhaps a thousand of his people.

The fragmenting of Sioux hegemony on the plains graphically illustrated the problems many Native American societies encountered while undergoing intense physical and cultural attrition in the United States and Canada. With a relatively sparse population and the lack of a sophisticated or durable commercial and industrial base the Sioux found it impossible to maintain an effective barrier against American and Canadian expansion. The Sioux, like other Indians, were entirely dependent upon the procurement of a select range of natural resources. Buffalo were particularly important, both as a material resource and a unifying social icon. Lacking modern technology, the Sioux relied on the technical and economic infrastructure of Britain and the United States for tools and implements, a relationship that grew more one-sided as the frontier was developed by whites. This dependency virtually nullified any hope of long-term resistance or of preserving Sioux society under conditions desired by headmen such as Sitting Bull.

Sitting Bull would try, as other Native Americans had before him, to circumvent these problems by building large confederacies among many tribes. Like the others, he would not be successful. Northern Plains Indians were unable to overcome traditional rivalries and differences—which whites often exploited—and competition intensified when game dwindled and unorganized land became scarce. The chances for a broad-based alliance declined in direct relation to the erosion of familiar resources.

These problems became acute for the Sioux refugees in Canada. Sitting Bull himself exemplified the conflicting issues and confusion that bedeviled his people. He wanted revenge but desired peace and security, and he seemed to recognize that the two were incompatible. Sitting Bull often expressed his patriotism and his longing to provide for the others, but his efforts were subverted by fear and ignorance among whites, among his own people, and in himself. Foresight failed him, his own inconsistencies made him vacillate, and his leadership suffered.

The Sioux hegira offers opportunities for comparative discourses on Canadian and American methods of extending control across contiguous, sparsely populated frontiers, and on the pattern of relations between the two nations on matters pertaining to the western half of the continent. In the upper levels of government in Washington, Ottawa, and London, discussion was marked by waffling and temporizing. Only Canadian officials gave the issue serious recognition, but only because it reflected upon important considerations of political autonomy from Great Britain and cultural and economic autonomy from the United States. In London, Her Majesty's government was more concerned with the state of British-American relations, fearing that a thousand Indians in a far corner of the Empire might upset rapprochement with a troublesome regional power. Some tendency existed on the part of the British government to sacrifice Dominion interests for such causes, or so many Canadians thought.

In the United States, the discussion over the Sioux in Canada was subsumed by party competition and "turf wars" within the federal bureaucracy, as the administration of Rutherford B. Hayes attempted to keep western interests, annexationists, Anglophobes, social reformers, army commanders, and Democrats in check. Reluctant executive departments shunted the problem back and forth. The State Department regarded the Sioux refugees as an "Indian problem," properly addressed by the Department of the Interior's Office of Indian Affairs. Interior strongly disagreed, pointing out that refugee issues involving other nations fell under the aegis of the Department of State, and that there was little precedent for Interior to approach foreign governments. A deadlock occurred, and the issue fell by default to the U.S. Army, whose commanders complained bitterly about having to patrol international borders in a wilderness with inadequate forces and no clear mission objectives. American policy devolved to stalling for time in the hope that the Canadian government would eventually take full responsibility for the Sioux.

It was a decision that the Dominion government refused to make. So seriously did they take this issue that Ottawa violated imperial procedure and sent its minister of the Interior to Washington, D.C., to negotiate directly with President Hayes, an act that caused considerable discomfort in the British Legation and in London. The talks resulted in an American commission to the Sioux, which failed. As herds of buffalo disappeared from the Northwest Territories, Canadian officials resorted to the rather barbaric policy of starving the Sioux in order to force their return across the border to prison, reservations, and a minimum dole of hard bread and dried meat.

It is a measure of the Dominion's institutions of government on the frontier that Ottawa was able to do this with minimum disturbances among the Sioux. The organization charged with maintaining order in the Territories was the North-West Mounted Police. The Police reflected the patterns and interests of Canadian political culture, just as the U.S. Army reflected those of the United States. Officials of the Dominion, a relatively new entity, wanted to establish a durable political identity. Order was imposed by design from a central source of authority and power, a very "British" model of imperial government. In the United States, the emphasis was upon growth and expansion. Laissez faire was the model, weak federalism the method, and order was an organic process often imposed more by social convention and the developing economic structure than by institutions of government.

These distinctive approaches resulted in markedly different methods of controlling the frontier. The U.S. Army followed no comprehensive strategy, beyond responding in force to a series of crises. Locations and complements of posts in the Trans-Mississippi West were usually determined by potential or recently concluded conflicts, or through the political influence of local special interests who desired lucrative government contracts to supply troops. Discrete campaigns were initiated after some incident occurred, and often fell apart when the "enemy" failed to materialize.[1]

In part, this lack of strategy resulted from widespread disinterest among military officers in campaigning and maintaining order on a contiguous frontier. Between the War of 1812 and Southern secession in 1860, a standard of professionalism had evolved, abetted by influential American strategists and teachers such as Dennis

[1] Robert Utley, *Frontier Regulars: The United States Army and the Indian, 1866–1891* (New York: Macmillan, 1973), chap 3.

Hart Mahan and Henry Wager Halleck. Mahan and Halleck had been deeply influenced by the work of the Swiss military historian Henri Jomini, who chronicled Napoleon Bonaparte's "strategies of annihilation." They borrowed heavily from Jomini, advocating offensive warfare and the concentration of forces against decisive points, designs consistent not with the defensive or policing traditions of a developing regional power but with the large armies of Europe. The Civil War reinforced such doctrines.[2]

A paradox evolved in the American military. The army that professional soldiers aspired to was European in character and in mission. But the army that existed after 1865 was very different: a coastal defense system, a government engineering corps, and a national police force. Organization and strategy were often delineated by officers on the basis of their ideals rather than real situations the army faced on the frontier. At West Point, cadets read about Napoleon at Austerlitz and Jena, but not about Bugeaud and the French colonial forces in Africa.

The U.S. Army never developed a cogent sense of mission in the West. Primarily an offensive instrument of limited use in circumstances calling for occupation and policing, it could do little but respond to crisis with blunt force. The very presence of soldiers, whose purpose the Indians clearly understood, often exacerbated disorder. As a result, American officials found their options severely limited by the inability to effectively use federal authority to solve problems on the frontier.

Between 1875 and 1890, the army maintained approximately 19,000 troops in the Trans-Mississippi West, at an annual average expense of between fifteen and twenty million dollars.[3] In the same period the North-West Mounted Police employed 500 officers and spent less money than the U.S. Army did in a single year.[4] Canadian militia units, totaling a little over 2000 troops, were fully mobilized just once, during Louis Riel's second rebellion in 1885. These figures say something about the differing patterns of settlement on the Canadian and American frontier. Justice and government in America were

[2] John Shy, "Jomini," and Russell F. Weigley, "American Strategy from its Beginnings Through the First World War," *in* Peter Paret, ed., *Makers of Modern Strategy: From Machiavelli to the Nuclear Age* (Princeton, N.J.: Princeton University Press, 1986), pp. 143–85, 413–18, and 436–37.

[3] Utley, *Frontier Regulars*, 15–16. See also U.S. Secretary of War, *Annual Reports*, for the years 1874 through 1890.

[4] R. G. MacLeod, *The North-West Mounted Police and Law Enforcement, 1872–1905* (Toronto: University of Toronto Press, 1976), chap 1. See also Canadian Parliament, *Sessional Papers*, "Report of the Commissioner of the Northwest Mounted Police" for the years 1884 through 1889.

often compromised by a burgeoning population and rapid, uncontrolled growth. In contrast, Canadian expansion was slow and subject to careful regulation. Pressure on native Canadian Indian ranges was less intense, resulting in less overall discord between the Dominion and the western tribes.[5]

On the other hand, the figures also say something about methods of control. The Mounted Police was a genuine police force, not an occupational army operating as a national posse. Its principal mission was the deterrence of disorder, necessary because the Dominion did not have the resources to commit large numbers of troops to contain crisis in the Northwest Territories. Its response to the Sioux hegira emphasized the relative success of such an approach, while Riel's rebellion demonstrated its limitations.

The Mounted Police was not just a law enforcement agency, but an entire legal system on horseback. Officers were granted extraordinary powers by the government in Ottawa to compensate for their small numbers and vast jurisdiction. They not only apprehended lawbreakers, but acted as magistrates, passing judgment and enforcing penalties. Their civil and legal authority in the Territories could not be challenged, and their interpretations of the law and the good of society were tantamount to fiat. The Police became symbols of order, justice, and national authority in a nation that coveted all three. They evolved a myth—not unfounded—of superb competence. It served them well, both in Ottawa and on the frontier, where psychology was an important tool of deterrence.

In addition to these advantages, the Mounted Police benefited from a substantial tradition of authority already established in the Northwest Territories. After the 1790s western Canada had been "managed" by a network of Hudson's Bay Company agents, who maintained commercial posts and a rough system of justice, since it was to the company's advantage to encourage order.[6]

Canada was able to implement a two-tiered system of control in the Territories: a trained, highly visible, paramilitary police force that used relatively nonviolent tactics of civil regulation and crisis deterrence, backed by an "invisible" military that could be mobilized in the event of an emergency. In the United States, the situation was in marked contrast: a highly visible, poorly trained army, a crazy-quilt

---

[5] Doug Owram, *Promise of Eden: The Canadian Expansionist Movement and the Idea of the West, 1856–1900* (Toronto: University of Toronto Press, 1980), 217–24, 227–34.

[6] An account of this system is found in E. E. Rich, *Hudson's Bay Company* (New York: Macmillan, 1960), vols. 2 and 3.

system of local justice and overlapping political venue, and no national police force specifically constituted for the frontier.[7]

The Mounted Police had been sent to the Territories to lay the foundation of a nation by ordering a vast region through law, allowing Canadian civilization, lacking in resources, to be introduced with a minimum of difficulties. The role of the U.S. Army is less clear. The American process of ordering the frontier was organic, not rational. Settlement brought law and civilization to the Trans-Mississippi West in a spontaneous fashion, and the army functioned less often as a vanguard than as a last resort, an attempt to solve problems already flaring into crisis.

Less obvious were the distinctions between United States and Canadian Indian policy during this period. The Dominion was in the midst of setting up a reservation system when the Sioux crossed the border; the elimination of large buffalo herds in the territories between 1876 and 1881 accelerated this process. Canada regarded the Sioux as a serious impediment to the stable transition of native populations on the plains to reservation life and assimilation, a view that contributed to the Dominion's relatively harsh actions after 1879.[8]

Border crossings by Native Americans and the Sioux hegira involved issues beyond sanctuary for a few thousand Indian refugees camped at Wood Mountain in the Northwest Territories. For the British, the dilemma lay in maintaining decent relations with a volatile regional rival. To the Canadians, nothing less than national survival seemed to be at stake; failure in the Territories might give the Americans or the Empire a chance to short-circuit the sovereign experiment. For the Americans, the issue had manifold political ramifications: maintenance of an adequate national armed force, jurisdictional struggles between local interests and the federal government over Native American policy, relations with Great Britain and Canada, resurgent annexationist sentiment, the developing economic structure in the West, and the day-to-day machinations of two national political parties.

Meanwhile, the Sioux lived and then began to starve at Wood Mountain.

---

[7] Such American law enforcement organizations as the U.S. Marshalls or the Texas Rangers might have served as a model for a national police force on the frontier, but they were usually restricted by numbers, resources, procedures, or by local jurisdictions.

[8] In 1914, the U.S. Board of Indian Commissioners sent a representative to Canada to study the reserve system. His report emphasized certain advantages of the Dominion's approach. See U.S. Board of Indian Commissioners, *The Administration of Indian Affairs in Canada: Report of an Investigation Made in 1914* [by Frederick H. Abbott, Secretary of the BIC]. (Washington, D.C., 1915).

CHAPTER 1

"Peace is much more fatal to Indians than war"

INITIAL MILITARY OPERATIONS IN
EASTERN MONTANA, 1876–1877

On July 5, 1876, during the nation's centennial celebration, word arrived from the western United States that a tribe of Indians had given America an unsavory birthday gift. On June 25, Lt. Col. George Armstrong Custer had led the Seventh Cavalry of the U.S. Army over a dry divide on the short-grass plains of eastern Montana, and down into the valley of the Little Bighorn River. There, his scouts had observed a huge encampment of Sioux Indians, along with numbers of Cheyenne and Arapaho. Custer, eager to redeem himself after his compromising testimony before a congressional investigation into the affairs of Secretary of War W. W. Belknap, took a gamble. He decided to attack quickly and hope the element of surprise would be enough to ensure a victory, or at least a disorderly retreat by the Indians.[1] The gamble did not pay off.

[1] Custer testified before a Congressional committee investigating scandals which involved Secretary of War W. W. Belknap and the administration of the stores sys-

In annihilating a cavalry regiment, the Sioux brought upon themselves a measure of infamy and a commitment of vengeance. But
they had a justifiable case. By the terms of the Fort Laramie treaty of
1868, the Black Hills of South Dakota were clearly a part of the Great
Sioux Reservation. By the winter of 1875–76 fifteen thousand white
miners entered the area seeking gold.[2] The United States government decided to ignore this intrusion, and take the area away from
the Sioux with a minimum of compensation.[3] Those Sioux who stayed
away from the reservation, hunting and gathering food in the empty
territory west of the Black Hills, were given an ultimatum to return
by January 31, 1876. The deadline came and went, and the sizable
number who did not return were declared "hostile" by the Department of the Interior. The Indians had little choice but to lose themselves in the Powder River country and resist attempts by the U.S.
Army to force them out. After the Custer debacle this "police-action"
assumed the proportions of a major war, at least to the newspapers.

Most Americans believed the chief instigator of hostilities to be
Sitting Bull, a Sioux warrior of some repute, a political leader of good
ability, and a religious functionary whose visions and power came,
he and his people believed, from a personal accord with a changing
universe. The white press often described him as intelligent, recal-
citrant, violent, and dangerous.[4] Perhaps because of these views,
Sitting Bull came to be the symbol of Sioux resistance on the Great
Plains, and the paramount leader among such rising names in the
national consciousness as Crazy Horse, Gall, Rain-in-the-Face, Young-
Man-Afraid-of-His-Horses, and Black Moon. "He defies the government," said Montana Congressional Representative Martin MacGinnis
in an interview with the New York Tribune, "and hopes that he can
get the Sioux nation to join him. If they will only do this, he promises
to drive the whites back into the sea, out of which they came."[5]

---

tem for the army. President Ulysses S. Grant was enraged by Custer's testimony and
refused to allow him to lead his regiment in the campaign against the Sioux that
summer. Only when Grant's friends, including Gen. William T. Sherman and Gen.
Philip Sheridan, interceded on Custer's behalf, did Grant change his mind. Custer's
reputation was tarnished and his ambitions were in jeopardy when he led his soldiers over the hills and into the valley of the Little Bighorn. He may have been looking for a dramatic victory to redeem himself. See Robert Utley, *Custer and the
Great Controversy* (Los Angeles: University of California Press, 1962).

[2] Robert Utley, *Frontier Regulars, 1866–1891* (New York: Macmillan, 1973),
247.

[3] Ibid., 248.

[4] Stanley Vestal, *Sitting Bull, Champion of the Sioux: A Biography* (Boston:
Houghton Mifflin, 1932), 91ff.

[5] "Sitting Bull's Bloody Career," *New York Tribune*, 7 May 1876.

The conflict came to be called "Sitting Bull's War," and when various units of the U.S. Army under Generals Alfred Terry and George Crook and Col. John Gibbon moved into the Powder River and Yellowstone River areas in the spring and summer of 1876, it was Sitting Bull's "Sioux Confederation" and not a loose amalgamation of tribes they would try to find. As MacGinnis told the Tribune:

> Of course Sitting Bull is anxious to confederate all the Sioux tribes and bands in a general war. . . . Of course the Government has no alternative except to bring him to terms. Any other course would be a cowardly and wicked surrender of our frontier settlers and our friendly Indian allies [to a] barbarous and determined enemy of our country.

Such statements, along with the intense media coverage given by ambitious newspaper editors, gave Sitting Bull an ominous reputation that inspired fear, hatred, admiration, even romance.[6]

An Indian of such apparent qualities, who seemed to resist the white man so successfully, was the subject of fascination for many Americans. Rumors sprang up, inevitably retold by the newspapers, concerning Sitting Bull's command of the English language; he supposedly had the skill of a linguist: he spoke German, French, and even Chinese fluently, in addition to several Indian languages. He was reportedly well-read, and could quote from Shakespeare and Melville. It was claimed that he had a finer military mind than any in the U.S. Army, and his "military successes" were evidence that he knew the tactical work of Caesar and Napoleon.[7]

Many anecdotes surfaced concerning Sitting Bull's origins, each attempting to explain his alleged capabilities. All were enhanced by the lack of reliable information concerning his life before 1865. Some reports described him as a white man displeased with white society and seeking revenge; others branded him a mixed-blooded genius, tired of the poor treatment afforded his people. One story claimed that he was an Ojibwa Indian of Canadian birth, a young man of great scholarly promise who had attended Saint John's College in

[6] Articles in the *New York Tribune*, the *New York Times*, the *New York Herald*, the *Chicago Times*, and Montana newspapers such as the *Helena Herald* and the *New North-West* "profiled" the career and character of Sitting Bull extensively. The obvious slant in these pieces is often invidious and sometimes racist. Among the Montana newspapers, some of the editorials were distinctly anxious in tone.

[7] Vestal, *Sitting Bull*, 91–99ff. Articles in various newspapers were ambivalent about Sitting Bull's origins, both ridiculing him and expressing a reserved admiration for his "talents."

Canada with the ambition of being a "big chief," and who had mysteriously disappeared in the early 1860s. This account was discredited by the discovery of the real Ojibwa, an alcoholic laborer living in a small village near Toronto, but not before the "news" had been reprinted across the United States and Canada, and generally accepted.[8]

These images and rumors seemed to create a formidable adversary for the U.S. Army in the summer of 1876. As the *New York Times* stated, "[Sitting Bull] sits calmly in the rear and directs the battle like a General."[9] In July of that year, with Crook's soldiers mauled on the Rosebud River and Custer's regiment dead on the slopes above the Little Bighorn River, it was Sitting Bull who received most of the notoriety. The events of the summer created a mystique, and the public's attention centered on Sitting Bull's "confederacy," even after the different Sioux tribes scattered or returned to the reservation.

Portrayed in this manner, Sitting Bull and the Sioux posed a problem for the government and those who supported reform of federal Indian policy. Education was thought to be the answer to the crisis in the West, along with "detribalization," assimilation, acculturation, and even the ultimate badge of civilization: property and capitalism.[10] But this "enlightened" view did not apply to nonreservation Indians who lived and hunted beyond the frontier. Public opinion was fickle, and changed with the circumstances. A single incident might engender sympathy or hatred for the Sioux. Newspaper coverage or reaction to events having nothing to do with the Sioux often influenced opinion.[11]

Nonreservation Indians threatened white society. The threat could be the expense of another Indian war, a blow to the pride and national spirit of Americans who believed in the superiority of the white race and the strength and goodness of American culture, the example set for reservation Indians, or the physical anxiety felt by citizens of the towns and mining camps on the western frontier. "Unless the Government takes prompt and vigorous measures to chastise the Sioux," the *New York Times* predicted, "the disaffection from this [the Berthold Indian Agency] and other friendly agencies will be enormous.[12] The Deer Lodge, Montana, *New North-West* also acknowledged rumors of discontent:

[8] "Sitting Bull," *Manitoba Daily Free Press*, 27 August 1877. Also, "Sitting Bull—Charley Jacobs," ibid., 29 September 1877.

[9] "The Last Indian Struggle," *New York Times*, 25 August 1876.

[10] Robert F. Berkhofer, Jr., *The White Man's Indian* (New York: Knopf, 1978), 166.

[11] Ibid., 25–30.

[12] "Several Indian Tribes Uneasy," *New York Times*, 9 July 1876.

A Sioux scout in the employ of the government at Fort Rice, after [the Little Bighorn], said he always knew the Sioux outnumbered the whites, and that he believed they would conquer in the end. This idea prevails to a great extent among the young warriors who go into a campaign better armed than the whites. . . . They are confident that they will win. Well informed river and frontiers-men insist that the Indians have an effective fighting force of at least 10,000, well-armed and abundantly supplied.[13]

Ten thousand well-armed Sioux, encouraged by the Custer debacle to believe that the white man's days were numbered—this was not a happy prospect for citizens on the frontier. Although it is not likely that there were ever as many as "10,000, well-armed and abundantly supplied," the figure and its implications were widely accepted. Anxiety in the region was founded upon misinformation, the same misinformation that influenced the perceptions and policies of the U.S. government.[14]

Nor were ten thousand well-armed Sioux warriors a happy prospect for the Office of Indian Affairs in Washington, D.C. Reformers and federal officials had been led to believe that the implementation of a benign "Peace Policy" toward the Indians—an attempt to "civilize and Christianize" them under the auspices of churches and religious organizations—was working well. The events of 1876 and after put the policy in jeopardy. In the political climate that followed Custer's defeat, Congress deadlocked over further reform legislation, and the American Indian reform movement came under vituperative attack.[15]

The changing tone of newspaper articles, editorials, and letters about reservation Indians indicated the shifting perceptions of the public before and after the Little Bighorn.[16] The changes demonstrated much concern, and the emotions generated by the conflict

[13] "The Indian Campaign," *New North-West*, 4 August 1876.

[14] Estimates of the number of Indians participating in the Little Bighorn vary. From the evidence concerning the events after the Little Bighorn, my own working assumption is that there were several thousand in the region, and perhaps not all were camped in the valley on that day.

[15] Gregory C. Thompson, "The Origins and Implementation of the American Indian Reform Movement: 1867–1912," (Ph.D. Diss., University of Utah, 1981), 101–2.

[16] The relation between the public and the media was synergistic. Newspapers created interpretations of material for public consumption, and public opinion often set the editorial parameters and working assumptions of writers, reporters, and editors. Occasionally, of course, a strong-willed editor or staff contradicted public opinion. See Marshall McLuhan, *Understanding Media* (New York: McGraw-Hill, 1964). Also, Daniel J. Boorstin, *The Image: A Guide to Pseudo-Events in America* (New York: Harper and Row, 1964).

seemed to be sharper. On June 27, 1876, two days after the Little Bighorn, but eight days before the nation received the news, an article in the *Helena Herald* published the following prediction about the fate of Sitting Bull and his people:

> Sitting Bull, thy doom is fast approaching. With three commands, at the heads of which the following well-known names appear—Terry, Gibbon, Custer, Crook, Brisbane, Ball, and others—we cannot see how you can escape. Better throw up thy hands, old boy, if thou wouldst see the close of this Centennial year. Your obituary notice, if it devolves on us, shall be arranged to suit the widow. There is no doubt but that the ball will soon open in earnest, and Montanans can rest assured that something will be done this time.[17]

On July 5, after word arrived of the battle, the Herald's attitudes had changed:

> Our little body of soldiers are sent out in a wilderness to cope with a foe a hundred times their number, as well-armed and mounted, and familiar with the ground, and, withal, the bravest fighting men that have ever been known in history. Perhaps the sacrifice of Custer was needed to wake the nation to the true nature of the war that was on hand.[18]

And after further reflection, the *Herald* offered a draconian solution to the "Indian problem":

> If this [Federal Indian] policy is to be continued longer we suggest that a part of the District of Columbia be set apart for a Sioux Reservation, and then under the eyes of Congress let the mooted question be settled of whether more Indians can be Christianized than white men scalped, tortured or murdered. . . . [The Indians] ought to be compelled to live within their reservations, the same as wild beasts confined to cages. If they cannot be forced to work and earn their own living they must be supported as paupers until they naturally die out.[19]

[17] "Indian Campaigns," *Helena Herald*, 27 June 1876.

[18] "Custer's Last Stand," *Helena Herald*, 5 July 1876.

[19] Untitled editorial, *Helena Herald*, 8 July 1876. Another Montana newspaper, the Fort Benton *Record*, had a different impression of the Custer debacle:

> Many commanders of far greater military ability than Custer ever possessed have been court-martialed and shot for similar offenses followed by less disastrous consequences; and if Custer had not died on the field he would undoubtedly have been tried and punished for his unpardonable breach of military discipline, and the people would have been as loud in his denunciation as they are now in his praise.
>
> —"The Yellowstone Slaughter," *Benton Record*, 14 July 1876.

In general, western newspapers and their readership exhibited a similar evolution of opinion. The certainty of victory was quickly replaced by shocked explanations for the Seventh Cavalry's defeat: the soldiers were too few in number and not well equipped, the terrain favored the Indians, and the Sioux were some of the finest warriors in the world, heavily armed by government agencies and trained in the art of war from birth. Finally, the inevitable finger was pointed. Federal policy toward Indians and the administration of the reservation system received the brunt of editorial cudgels. During this phase, virulent rhetoric against Indian character often made editorial arguments indecipherable. Native Americans were portrayed as degraded savages, cunning in their deceit and skillful at wreaking cruel havoc on innocents. The Indians supposedly had deceived the federal government, especially the Office of Indian Affairs and the agents of the reservation system. The *New North-West*'s sarcastic description of "The Youth of Sitting Bull" is one example of this kind of rhetoric:

> We used to give him a truthful little hatchet and a butcher knife and the old yellow cat all for to play with. I should judge by that he must have scalped that old cat as much as sixteen or seventeen hundred times before he was three years old . . . and then to see him draw rations and blankets and things just in play! Why I have seen him walk around the tepee hour after hour and everytime he would come up and answer to a different name and draw acorns for rations and burdock leaves for blankets and fish bones for scalping knives.[20]

White populations in the West perceived a great deal to gain by the demise of the Indian and much to lose if Indians continued to move about beyond the reservations. Nowhere was this more true than in Montana and the Dakotas, where the Black Hills were believed to be brimming with gold, the Rocky Mountains held valuable minerals, the hides of the region's diminishing buffalo herds brought quick money, and the grass of the eastern plains could support cattle. Western "boosterism" also affected white perceptions of Native Americans. Indians "hanging around," especially "hostile" ones, worried local businessmen, entrepreneurs, newspaper editors, and politicians. An Indian war would impart an unpopular image to the region, and many citizens predicted a drop in immigration, government and commercial building projects, and local business profits.[21] The twin motives

[20]"The Youth of Sitting Bull," *New North-West*, 15 September 1876.
[21] At the same time army officers were accusing western interests of encouraging and in some cases fomenting Indian wars in order to realize profits from supplying military units in the field against the Indians. See Utley, *Frontier Regulars*, 46–47.

of profit and security generated an outcry against the Sioux in Montana, and started many rumors. Unfortunately, Westerners often believed the stories they themselves spread.

For newspapers in the East, an Indian war like that on the Montana plains in 1876 was a windfall. The Powder River campaigns provided an entertaining diversion from more conventional stories about events in the cities or the latest dispatches from the war between Russia and the Ottoman Empire.[22] Editors often posted news of the Sioux war in prominent positions in their newspapers, and readers responded well.[23]

Eastern newspapers were generally milder and more urbane than their western counterparts in their descriptions of western conflicts. Articles and editorials were not quite so confident of initial victory and were quicker to point out how injustice and the problems of the reservation system often created violence between Indians and whites. But general opinions about Indians remained the same: they were warlike, white-hating barbarians who rejected the benefits of western civilization for a violent, primitive life. The difference between the editorial stance in the East and the West seemed to be the degree of subtlety and finesse. The *New York Times* expressed the following opinion about white miners in the Black Hills, for example:

> From that unwarranted invasion the present difficulties have gradually sprung up, so that an expedition that originally cost a hundred thousand dollars perhaps, must lead to an expenditure of millions, which will advance civilization in no way, except by the destruction of the uncivilized.[24]

Yet, in the same article, the *Times* asserted that "the Sioux live by chase and feed chiefly upon flesh."

[22] Long-standing disagreements between Czarist Russia and the Ottoman Empire had erupted into armed conflict in early 1876. Newspapers in Montana strongly supported the Russians, but the sentiment seemed less motivated by the Russian cause than by negative opinions about the Ottoman Empire's ally, Great Britain. Apparently there was strong anti-British sentiment in Montana at the time. It may have been a residue from the bad feeling several years before, when the North-West Mounted Police cleared the Northwest Territories of American traders. The *Benton Record* and the *Helena Herald* complained bitterly when the police tried and imprisoned four Americans in 1875. But officers of the police often visited Fort Benton and Helena while on leave, and did much to repair the force's image. By 1877, both the *Record* and the *Herald* complimented James Macleod, A. G. Irvine, James Walsh, and other officers who visited Fort Benton and Helena occasionally.

[23] The front pages of the *New York Times*, the *New York World*, and the *New York Tribune*, for May through September, 1876, will confirm this. Similar editorial methods were used during many conflicts with Indians; the Nez Perce conflict of 1877 is another example.

[24] "The Causes and Consequences," *New York Times*, 7 July 1876.

"Feeding on the flesh" seemed to be a common theme among those who disdained the Sioux Indians, especially in the Northern Plains and Rocky Mountain regions. Except for the occasional army officer, some local church groups, and those few citizens who were affiliated with the Indian reform movement, most Montanans seemed to agree with the editor of the *Helena Herald*, who suggested: "[Turn] them over to Russia to fight the Bashi Bazouks, or to Egypt to employ in its war against Abyssinia. . . . It would give the Indian an occupation suited to his taste."[25] If soldiering did not work, the *Herald* had another suggestion:

> Peace is much more fatal to Indians than war. A good season of measles or small pox will accomplish more than all our troops under the best leadership. It is cheaper, wiser, safer and more humane to kill Indians with kindness than in warfare . . . even if we have to fence in parks and stock them with game, or build coloseums [*sic*] and amphitheaters and stock them with wild beasts, gamefowls or even gladiators for their daily entertainment.[26]

Other Montana newspapers were not quite so rabid, but their sentiments were often similar.

Rabid or not, Montanans and residents of neighboring states and territories clamored for more military protection, and with a few notable exceptions, public opinion in the East approved.[27] Actions were taken in haste in the aftermath of the Little Bighorn. Congress approved funds for two forts in the Yellowstone River valley, the center of Sioux activity—a project that the commanding General of the Army William T. Sherman had been advocating for years. Congress also authorized enlistment of twenty-five hundred additional cavalry soldiers.[28] The army was also given authority to disarm the reservation Indians of the agencies in South Dakota. The move was supposed to prevent violence, but its net effect was to make Indians more dependent upon government annuities and subsidies, for without firearms they could not hunt and joining the Sioux in Montana would be very difficult. Certain Indian reformers charged that the army's intent was to starve these Indians into submission.[29]

Criticism of the government's policy grew as the conflict in Montana dragged on. The army's initial success against the Sioux

[25] "Pastoral Life of Indians," *Helena Herald*, 24 May 1876.

[26] "Wants an Offer," *Helena Herald*, 20 July 1876.

[27] Exceptions were the staff of the Indian Office and certain officers of the army.

[28] *Congressional Record*, 44th Cong. 1st sess., 15 August 1876, 5674–75 and 5694–96.

[29] U.S. Commissioner of Indian Affairs, *Annual Report, 1876*, 411.

was unsatisfactory. When Col. Nelson A. Miles stepped off the gang-plank of the steamer "Durfee" and onto the muddy embankment of the Yellowstone River in late July, he was not happy with what he saw. In a letter to his wife, he complained about Gen. Alfred Terry's troops:

> I must say that I found matters entirely different from what I expected. I never saw a command so completely stampeded as this, either in the volunteer or regular service, and I believe without reason . . . this campaign thus far would not have been creditable to a militia.[30]

Terry's command had recently finished burying the bodies of the Seventh Cavalry. Word of Crook's defeat on the Rosebud had arrived. As Nelson Miles's Fifth Infantry and additional reinforcements unloaded from steamers at the mouth of the Rosebud, a pall of anxiety was immediately discernible among the bivouac. Characteristically, Miles favored immediate and economical action, and was blunt in his criticism of Terry and Col. John Gibbon. "I hope I may get the chance," he wrote to his wife, "as I would willingly undertake this affair with one third the number of troops now in the field."[31] Various officers in the encampment voiced similar sentiments.[32]

It was a divided and fearful command that finally moved up the Rosebud on August 8 in search of the Sioux. Terry knew that Crook's column was somewhere south of him, and he had a vague plan to sandwich the Indians between the two commands and crush them without unacceptable losses. The problem with Terry's plan was that no one knew where anyone else was. Crook was "somewhere south." The Sioux were "in the vicinity."

On the morning of August 10, frightened scouts came riding back into the night camp with reports of large numbers of Indians approaching fast from the south. Terry quickly deployed his nervous troops into a defensive formation, and everyone waited for the onslaught. Then a lone horseman appeared riding down the Rosebud Valley. He was William F. Cody and he bore messages from Crook, whose column the scouts had mistaken for the Sioux. The Indians had vanished.

Later, a large trail was discovered leading east, toward the Dakota reservations. After much discussion, Terry and Crook decided

---

[30] Virginia W. Johnson, *The Unregimented General: A Biography of Nelson A. Miles* (Boston: Houghton-Mifflin, 1962), 93–94.

[31] Ibid., 95–96.

[32] Utley, *Frontier Regulars*, 269.

to unite their commands and follow.[33] Miles and the Fifth Infantry were ordered north to hold the fords of the Yellowstone River against any Sioux who might splinter off from the main group and cross into the Big Dry of east-central Montana—a place of rolling flats, crumbling buttes and hills, and steep ravines that could easily hide large groups of Indians. Miles continued to be unimpressed with the campaign:

> On the tenth we met Crook's command making one of his magnificent scouts, as senseless and ill-advised as it was fruitless. . . . He had not the remotest chance of catching the Indians. . . . Everybody hopes the Indians will be so good as to return to their Agencies, which would surely be a great accommodation to us and spare us much embarrassment.[34]

Terry and Crook trudged through rainstorms and mud for another week and bivouacked on the mouth of the Powder River. Disgusted with the slow progress of the columns, Crook's Shoshoni scouts deserted, riding home to the Wind River valley. Cody also departed, and discontent among the officers and soldiers grew.

Bad feeling in the field was mirrored by rising criticism of the campaign among the news media. It was generally reported that Terry and Crook couldn't find the Sioux, and several items appeared in newspapers that cast doubts upon the army's hopes for success. The *New York Tribune* reported that a message from Sitting Bull made it clear that the Sioux would only return to the reservations if the whites were removed from the Black Hills.[35] The *Tribune* also stated that large numbers of reservation Sioux were slipping away to "join Sitting Bull."[36]

In early August, several newspapers including the Deer Lodge, Montana, *New North-West* reported that emissaries from the Sioux had offered tribes in Canada—Canadian Sioux, the Blackfeet, Cree, and Assiniboine—an alliance against whites of the United States and the Dominion. The Canadian Indians refused the offer, but the editor of the *New North-West* was anxious. After reminding its readers that the tribes north of the border numbered 12,400 warriors, the newspaper worried: "If they were to join the tribes now fighting the United States, nothing on this side of the line could prevent them."[37] Con-

---

[33] U.S. Secretary of War, *Annual Report, 1876*. 45th Cong. 2d sess., vol. 1, "Report of the General in Command of the Army," "Report of the Brigadier General in Command of the Department of the Missouri," 488.

[34] Johnson, *Unregimented General*, 101–3.

[35] "The North-West War," *New York Tribune*, 15 July 1876.

[36] "The War With the Sioux," *New York Tribune*, 8 July 1876.

[37] "Sioux Diplomats at Work," *New North-West*, 4 August 1876.

currently, the Fort Benton *Record* received news from Fort Walsh in the Northwest Territories of Canada that six hundred lodges of American Yankton Sioux were camped thirty miles away, "making mischief."[38]

Meanwhile, the rain abated and Terry and Crook continued to slog eastward along with two thousand troops, following the trail of the Sioux. The trail had diminished since they had left the Rosebud valley, and the two generals surmised correctly that the Indians were scattering into small groups. Events at the fords of the Yellowstone supported their guess. On August 23, a detached company of the Fifth Infantry at the mouth of Glendive Creek fired on several bands of Indians crossing the Yellowstone toward the north. Colonel Miles hurried to the ford with reinforcements, and when Terry received the news, he split his command from Crook's and raced down Glendive Creek. By the time Miles and Terry arrived, the last Indians had disappeared into the ravines and bluffs of the Big Dry. On September 1, Terry once more sat on the banks of the Yellowstone, contemplating his next move.

Time had restored Terry's confidence. On the 27th of August, as his command dashed down the Glendive, he sent a message to General Sheridan, informing his departmental commander that both his and Crook's commands were "strong enough to encounter the Indians separately." Terry proposed that the soldiers on the Yellowstone operate against any Indians found north of the river.[39]

Eventually the trail that Crook followed disappeared, and bereft of supplies the troops pushed on a starvation march toward Custer City in the Dakotas. On the way they found the Sioux and the Sioux found them: as the vanguard of Crook's column struck a Sioux camp near Slim Buttes on September 14, the main force was attacked by Sioux warriors led by Crazy Horse. The engagement cost Crook nothing except a large number of mules, but it further demoralized his hungry soldiers.[40]

By early September, Sheridan concluded that new tactics were needed. The Indians were scattered. Sitting Bull's people were probably north of the Yellowstone, and Crazy Horse and a large number of Sioux were to the southeast around the Black Hills. The remaining Indians were reported to be moving slowly back onto the reservations. Crook's and Terry's commands were exhausted and disorga-

[38] "Fort Walsh," *Benton Record*, 4 August 1876. The estimate is probably an exaggeration. But it serves to illustrate growing anxiety among whites about an alliance between Plains Indians on both sides of the border.

[39] U.S. Secretary of War, *Annual Report, 1876.* "Report of the General of the Army," 37.

[40] Ibid.

nized, and the season was late. Winter would soon close down operations. Sheridan ordered Terry to establish a temporary cantonment at the mouth of the Tongue River on the Yellowstone. Miles's Fifth Infantry, reinforced by six companies of the Twenty-Second Infantry, would garrison the valley of the Yellowstone until spring allowed a renewed campaign. Questions arose about the orders for this garrison; Miles wanted authorization to conduct winter forays against the Sioux, but Terry stated that the command was only to hold the Yellowstone in the vicinity of the Tongue River.[41] Terry's soldiers pulled out for the Dakotas in mid-September, and, according to Miles, "The country was then left practically in the possession of the Indians."[42]

To the outside world, these developments did not provide a satisfying conclusion. The American public had been led to expect a war in the conventional sense of the word—the army pitted in battle against an alliance of Indians led by Sitting Bull. When the campaign fizzled out, puzzlement and disgust ensued. The *New North-West* editorialized:

> We hardly know how to account for the present state of affairs. Terry and Crook had each about two thousand troops. Sitting Bull was estimated to have at least 5,000 warriors, and had the two commands separated. It was believed that his warriors were brave and his chiefs skillful. Why did he not attack one column or the other? Why did he permit them to unite? Why did he run?

The newspaper proposed two possible explanations: either Sitting Bull and the Sioux would make a final stand in the Dakota Badlands, using the rough terrain to their advantage, or the alliance had broken apart. The "summer warriors" were returning to the reservations "to live off the government," while Sitting Bull and the "irreconcilables" might look for sanctuary in Canada.[43]

A week later, wonder had turned to antipathy. The editor of the *New North-West* wrote:

> Was there ever a more ludicrous ending to war inaugerated [sic] so dramatically? It reminds one of the old rhyme: "The King of France with twice ten thousand men / Did march his army up a hill and then marched down again.". . . And Sitting Bull! The Great Napoleonic Bovine upon whom "the eyes of Maryland" and half the world were centered to see . . . Bull the intrepid and dauntless, against whose

---

[41] Ibid., "Report of Brigadier-General Alfred H. Terry," 468.

[42] Nelson A. Miles, *Serving the Republic* (New York: Harper and Brothers, 1911), 146.

[43] "News From the Front," *New North-West*, 25 August 1876.

prowress [*sic*] the worst could be said was that he studied the Art of War wrong end foremost and run off after he won his victories.[44]

Several commentators predicted that Sitting Bull would lead the bulk of the nonreservation Sioux into Canada, where he could obtain arms and ammunition, shelter and subsistence, and a haven from which to raid into Montana. "If ten thousand Indians can defy and baffle this government," the *New North-West* concluded, "the Centennial is not as large a thing as we had believed."

By late September Miles's soldiers had nearly completed the Tongue River cantonment, a collection of crude wooden barracks and blockhouses chinked with mud and roofed with sod, tarps, and scraps of wood. The weather turned cold, and steamers loaded with supplies could no longer paddle up the Yellowstone because of low water. When reconnaissance patrols into eastern Montana from Fort Lincoln stopped after the first snowfall, the Tongue River cantonment was virtually isolated. For a time there was comparative peace, as the Sioux made their own preparations for winter. But on October 3, raiders from camps to the north tried to steal the cantonment's horses and pack-mules. Sentries drove them off, but not before several Indians riddled Miles's tent with bullets.[45]

The raid on the cantonment herds was a prelude to more serious action about a week later. For some time wagon trains loaded with supplies pushed overland from Fort Buford, at the confluence of the Yellowstone and Missouri Rivers, to Tongue River. On the evening of October 10 a train of ninety-five wagons escorted by four companies of soldiers under Capt. Charles W. Miner made camp on the Yellowstone, upstream from Glendive Creek. Miner was worried; signal fires had been seen on ridge crests and bluffs all day long.

At three o'clock in the morning an unknown number of Indians attacked the camp. Although there were no casualties, forty-seven mules were later counted missing—a serious handicap for the train. By six o'clock, Miner's train moved on. Throughout the morning the Sioux skirmished sporadically with the train's rearguard. At midday large numbers of Indians were sighted in the deep ravine of Clear Creek, and Miner decided to turn the train around and return to a temporary encampment at Glendive Creek.[46]

On October 13, the troops at Glendive Creek tried again. This time five companies under Lt. Col. E. S. Otis escorting eighty-six wag-

---

[44] "The Retreat of Sitting Bull," ibid., 1 September 1876.

[45] Nelson A. Miles, *Personal Recollections of General Nelson A. Miles* (Chicago: Werner Company, 1896), 222.

[46] U.S. Secretary of War, *Annual Report, 1876.* "Report of the General of the Army," 486–87.

ons started up the Yellowstone River toward the Tongue River cantonment. On the morning of the fifteenth, Otis's train came under attack at Spring Creek. Forming a thin skirmish line in front, Otis drove west to Clear Creek, where several hundred Sioux were spotted on the bluffs above. Ahead, the prairie had been set on fire. The soldiers pushed the Indians off the bluffs, but the number of Sioux in the area continued to increase. The Indians skirmished with the escort guarding the train for several miles beyond Clear Creek, until Otis ordered a camp made in a depression in the midst of a high, grassy plateau, leeward of a low ridge. Throughout the night, snipers hit the camp, but Otis was a stubborn person, and on the morning of the sixteenth the train again moved up the Yellowstone River.

Within hours Otis received a message from Sitting Bull:

> I want to know what you are doing travelling on this road. You scare all the buffalo away. I want to hunt on the place. I want you to turn back from here. If you don't I will fight you again. I want you to leave what you have got here, and turn back from here. I am your friend, Sitting Bull
>
> I mean all the rations you have got and some powder. Wish you would write as soon as you can.[47]

Sitting Bull's offer was clear: in return for the wagons, the soldiers were promised safe conduct back the way they had come. Otis informed Sitting Bull by note that he had nothing to say except that he "intended to take the train through."

Again the train moved forward, under constant fire from Indians atop the surrounding hills, bluffs, and plateaus. A short time later, the troops saw a white flag in the distance. Soon afterward, a meeting was arranged between Otis and "three of the principal soldiers of Sitting Bull." The emissaries told the colonel that the army's wagons were driving away the buffalo, that the Sioux people were hungry and angry, but desired to conclude peace with the soldiers. Otis replied that he had no authority to conclude anything with anyone, but Colonel Miles did. If they wanted to visit the colonel at the Tongue River cantonment, Otis would guarantee their safety with "the word of an officer."[48]

The Sioux emissaries politely declined, but promised to show up at Tongue River after visiting Fort Peck on the Missouri River. At first, Otis refused to give them rations, but "finally offered them as a

[47] Ibid., "Report of Lt. Colonel E.S. Otis," 516.
[48] Ibid., 517. Otis remarked that Sitting Bull seemed "unwilling to trust his person within our reach." However, Otis himself had been unwilling to meet Sitting Bull "outside the Lines," perhaps for similar reasons.

present one hundred and fifty pounds of hard bread and two sides of bacon." The train lumbered on and the Sioux disappeared.

Toward the evening of October 18, Otis's train met up with Miles and the entire Fifth Infantry camped on Custer Creek. The colonel received word of the attacks on the wagon trains from scouts, and set out immediately "to pursue Sitting Bull."[49] When Otis told him he would find the main Sioux camp either near the mouth of Cabin Creek or moving toward Fort Peck, Miles decided to move to Cherry Creek and then await Otis's return with the escort before pursuing the Indians further.

The regiment ran into the Sioux between Cherry and Cedar creeks and Miles immediately gave orders to engage them.[50] As the soldiers approached the head of a broad ravine, groups of warriors appeared on the surrounding bluffs. Estimating that there were about a thousand Indians, Miles deployed his four hundred troops in a defensive formation.[51] But Sitting Bull again wanted to parley. Under darkening skies that threatened the season's first heavy snowfall, he and Miles met on the flat before the bluffs. The colonel was suspicious; the night before he had dreamed of being struck in the forehead by a bullet, and wondered if it was some sort of portent.[52]

Sitting Bull wanted to know why the soldiers had not returned to the Missouri River to spend the season in their forts. He wanted what Miles termed "an old-fashioned peace for the winter," and promised that the Sioux would not fire on the soldiers if they left the area. He also hoped to trade for ammunition.[53]

Miles replied that the soldiers were in the Yellowstone valley to bring Sioux back onto the reservations. Only when the Indians surrendered their arms and were escorted to the Tongue River cantonment would there be peace. Sitting Bull refused to surrender. The sun set as the meeting broke up. Miles and Sitting Bull agreed to speak again the following day.[54]

Early the next morning, Miles jockeyed his troops into a better position, moving the regiment between the Sioux camp and a possible escape route north into the Big Dry. Sitting Bull appeared soon after the move was completed, and again he and Miles rode out

[49] Ibid., "Report of General Nelson A. Miles," 482.

[50] Ibid., "Report of Lt. Colonel E.S. Otis," 517.

[51] Miles, *Personal Recollections*, 223. Also, U.S. Secretary of War, *Annual Report, 1876.* "Report of General Nelson A. Miles," 482–83.

[52] Johnson, *Unregimented General*, 118.

[53] U.S. Secretary of War, *Annual Report, 1876.* "Report of General Nelson A. Miles," 483.

[54] Ibid., 484.

between the lines of soldiers and Sioux. Accompanying Sitting Bull were Bull Eagle, Pretty Bear, John Sans Arc, Standing Bear, White Bull, and Gall, who had spent much of the night arguing about whether to give up or fight. The militant faction had prevailed.

Sitting Bull was anxious to have peace, but unwilling to lose face in front of his people. He told Miles that he wanted to trade, especially for ammunition, but did not want annuities or government rations. He preferred to "live as an Indian." His words were lost on Miles. In the colonel's opinion, Sitting Bull "gave no assurance of good faith." Miles told the Sioux headman that refusing to surrender would be considered "an act of hostility." There was nothing more to say.

In the engagement that followed, Miles quickly took the offensive. The Sioux positioned themselves across the broken ground in front of their camp, but before it could be taken down, the defenders were driven off. Fleeing down Bad Route Creek, the Indians were forced to abandon lodges, clothing and implements, weapons, and large amounts of foodstores collected for the winter. The Fifth Infantry pursued them for forty-two miles, sporadically clashing with groups of warriors.

Eventually, the Indians left the soldiers behind. By the time they crossed the Yellowstone River on October 24, the majority of the Sioux wanted to surrender. After a night of bitter debate, the camp split along tribal lines, with the Sans Arcs and Miniconjous deciding to return to the Cheyenne River agency in the Dakotas. Sitting Bull and Gall and the militant faction of Hunkpapas packed up and started toward Fort Peck the next morning.

Miles caught up with the Sans Arc and Miniconjou Sioux the following day. Their leader, a young headman named Bull Eagle, quickly surrendered and informed the colonel that he intended to take his people to Cheyenne River. Miles was in a difficult position: if he accepted Bull Eagle's surrender, he would have the logistical problem of escorting over 1700 Indians back to the Tongue River cantonment, where they would have to be fed and sheltered. Instead, he decided to let the Sioux go on to Cheyenne River, and gave them a written note guaranteeing their safety and protection for thirty-five days, so long as they were moving in the general direction of the reservations. He took five headmen as hostages in return, including Bull Eagle. Later, he sent the five men with an escort to the headquarters of the Department of the Dakota in Minnesota, with a letter to General Terry explaining the situation. "I consider this the beginning of the end," he wrote, and added that "while we have sought and routed these people and driven them away from their ancient homes, I cannot but feel regret that they are compelled to submit to starvation."[55]

Humanitarian concerns did not interfere with Miles's recommendations for action during the winter. The prompt surrender and willing cooperation of the Sans Arc and Miniconjou Sioux led him to some hopeful, if naive, conclusions. "If we can keep [the Sioux] divided and destroy Sitting Bull's influence," Miles wrote to Terry, "I think we can end this trouble in time. Sitting Bull's band is the wildest on the continent." Miles concluded that the Sioux headman's resolve was wavering: "I believe Sitting Bull would be glad to make peace, but he is afraid he has committed an unpardonable offense."

In response to a note from Miles, Col. William B. Hazen and four companies of the Sixth Infantry boarded a steamer at Fort Buford and traveled up the Missouri River to the Indian agency at Fort Peck. At the agency, Assiniboines and Yanktonnais told Hazen that Sitting Bull and thirty lodges were on Dry Fork, twenty miles to the south. They expected to be joined by Iron Dog, leading a hundred lodges of Fort Peck Indians. The Sioux were destitute, and Hazen concluded that they no longer posed a threat. After seizing caches of ammunition at the agency and at Wolf Point, he left a company of troops on the reservation and returned to Fort Buford.[56]

Miles was less sanguine. The Fifth Infantry returned to the Tongue River Cantonment on November 3. Two days later the regiment marched north again into the Big Dry. This time the colonel used a strategy that had worked well for him in Texas during the Red River war of 1874: he divided his command into three columns with separate but contiguous areas of operation. Throughout November and December, the columns swept back and forth across the Montana plains from the north bank of the Milk River to the south bank of the Yellowstone. The weather that winter was severe. Blizzards pounded the troops, often three or four times a week. Temperatures dropped below −50°F and gale-force winds ripped across the high prairies. Fogs of ice crystals obscured the land by day, and the night skies were lit by brilliant displays of aurora borealis.

Only once did they find the Sioux. On December 7 a contingent under Lt. Frank Baldwin picked up a trail and fought a series of running skirmishes with hunting parties in the area. On the 18th, Baldwin's troops struck Sitting Bull's encampment of 122 lodges at Red Water. When the Sioux fled, the soldiers captured the camp and burned great quantities of stores. But they failed to rout the Indians,

[55] Ibid., 484–85.
[56] Ibid., "Report of General W. B. Hazen," 481–82.

who straggled south across the Yellowstone.[57] The column returned to the Tongue River cantonment on December 23, after marching 716 miles in a little over a month. Miles's and Capt. Simon Snyder's units had returned during the previous week. Miles's soldiers had walked 408 miles. Snyder's troops walked 308 miles.[58]

Other Indians in the Yellowstone valley occupied the Fifth Infantry through the rest of the winter. A delegation from various camps in the Powder River country had approached the cantonment in the fall, only to be set upon and slaughtered by the regiment's Crow scouts. After that, the Indians conducted a series of raids and feints against the cantonment, designed to draw the soldiers up the Tongue River and into an ambush. In December, Miles received word that these camps had coalesced into a large encampment of five hundred lodges on the headwaters of the Tongue. Among them were Oglalas and Teton Sioux led by Crazy Horse, some Cheyennes under Dull Knife, and a few Sans Arcs and Miniconjous who had surrendered to the regiment in October and later abandoned the trek back to the reservations.[59]

A few days after Christmas, Miles moved the Fifth Infantry and elements of the Twenty-Second Infantry south toward the headwaters of the Tongue River. On January 7 and 8, the soldiers fought a pitched battle with the Indians, assaulting their positions on a bluff after a sporadic barrage of artillery fire from several Napoleon guns. The engagement aborted in a driving blizzard, and the Indians escaped to the south across the frozen plains toward the Big Horn Mountains. Again they left large amounts of stores and equipment, which Miles ordered burned.

Further operations were curtailed by severe weather and supply problems. Feeling frustrated, Miles sent letters to his superiors, complaining that the chance for an early victory had been wasted because of bad logistics and lack of support from the army command. In an angry letter to William T. Sherman, he stated:

> Now if I have not earned a command I never will and if I have not given proof of my ability to bring my command into a successful encounter with Indians everytime I never will, besides I now have better knowledge of this country than any other white man and unless you can give me a command it should be no less than a department you can order my regiment out of this country as soon as you like for

[57] U.S. Commissioner of Indian Affairs, *Annual Report, 1877*, 412.

[58] Utley, *Frontier Regulars*, 274. Also, John C. Finerty, *War Path and Bivouac or the Conquest of the Sioux* (Norman, Okla.: University of Oklahoma Press, 1965; reprint of 1890 ed.), 226.

[59] Utley, *Frontier Regulars*, 276.

I have been campaigning long enough for the benefit of thieves and contractors.[60]

To his wife, Miles wrote: "I receive no more support from Department Headquarters than I do from Sitting Bull."[61]

Despite his attitude, Sherman and General Sheridan recognized that the intense, moody, and arrogant colonel possessed skills in frontier warfare perhaps unsurpassed in the army. His difficult personality and the rigid military seniority system would delay Miles's brigadier's star for several years, but he was given essentially what he wanted when Sherman created the District of the Yellowstone that winter. The district was as large as a department, and the military complement included two and a half cavalry regiments, two and a half infantry regiments, and a battalion of Pawnee scouts. Miles had more autonomy than any other colonel in the army; he could operate against Indians regardless of command boundaries, and could requisition supplies and replacements without going through normal departmental channels. In effect, Sherman and Sheridan put Miles on the front line, while relegating his immediate superiors, Terry and Crook, to administrative positions.

Miles worked a lasting impression on Sitting Bull. The colonel broke the traditional winter cessation of hostilities, and the Sioux could not shake him. "Bearcoat," as the Indians called Miles for the fur-collared coat he habitually wore, seemed to be everywhere at once. He was on the Yellowstone River in October, pushing wagon trains up to his post. He stormed through the Big Dry later the same month, burning Sitting Bull's encampment and chasing the warriors across the river. Then he caught up with them again, and split the tribes apart. More soldiers appeared at Fort Peck, forcing the Sioux to move south, and in December he captured and burned Sitting Bull's camp a second time. Miles and his troops destroyed Crazy Horse's encampment on the Tongue River a few days before Sitting Bull arrived to visit.[62]

Worst of all, the Sioux had lost their shelters, food stores, and equipment, and were facing a winter of starvation and exposure. The soldiers showed no evidence of vacating the Yellowstone country, and work on the Tongue River cantonment proceeded even during the coldest months. The approaching spring would bring renewed campaigns against the Indians. In addition to Miles's infantry units sitting in the middle of the traditional buffalo hunting ranges, patrols from the south and east increased. Col. Ranald Mackenzie led sev-

[60] Library of Congress, "William T. Sherman papers," 20 January 1877.
[61] Johnson, *Unregimented General*, 155.
[62] Utley, *Frontier Regulars*, 278.

eral forays through the western Dakotas, and Crook's troops from the Department of the Platte stepped up operations in Wyoming.

Sitting Bull realized that the whites held him responsible for the battle at the Little Bighorn. Apparently, he believed that he could not surrender, for the soldiers would imprison or kill him. He was convinced that if he stayed out on the Montana plains, Miles would pursue him relentlessly, and his people would slowly give out and desert him, one by one.[63] The constant pressure began to have an effect on the morale of those Indians remaining off the reservations. By this time the militant factions in the Sioux and Cheyenne camps had been discredited by repeated attacks at unexpected times and places. By February most of the Indians believed that the war could not be won. Reservation Indians visited in the camps throughout January and February with peace offers from the federal government. Even though the offers amounted to nothing more than a demand for unconditional surrender, small groups of Sioux turned up at the Missouri River reservations, seeking food and shelter.

In February 1877, General Crook convinced a respected Brulé Sioux headman named Spotted Tail to negotiate with the remaining Indians. At Spotted Tail's insistence, Crook relaxed the government's terms of surrender: the Indians would have to surrender their horses and guns, which would be returned to them later. Crook also promised to use his influence to set up a Sioux and Cheyenne reservation in the Yellowstone–Powder River region.[64]

When he learned of Spotted Tail's mission, Miles was angered by what he believed to be a blatant attempt to steal credit for ending the Sioux war. He modified his own terms of surrender and sent several emissaries to report on the kind treatment and generous provisions available to those who chose to turn themselves in at the Tongue River cantonment.[65] With surrender merely a matter of time, the negotiations quickly degenerated into a contest between Crook and Miles over who would claim a threadbare victory. In the end, Spotted Tail's prestige was the crucial factor. Over three thousand Indians surrendered to Crook's troops at the reservations in the early spring;

---

[63] In both of his autobiographies, *Personal Recollections* and *Serving the Republic*, Miles's account of his meetings with Sitting Bull reflect the distrust and ill-feeling both had for the other. Miles, writing in the 1890s, described the headman in a stereotypical light: cunning, deceitful, harsh, and ruthless. In contrast, he admired Joseph of the Nez Perces and the Comanche leader, Quannah Parker. Sitting Bull's actions while in exile in Canada demonstrated similar opinions about Miles.

[64] U.S. Secretary of War, *Annual Report, 1877,* "Report of General George Crook," 84–86.

[65] George E. Hyde, *Spotted Tail's Folk: A History of the Brulé Sioux* (Norman: University of Oklahoma Press, 1961), 237–47.

barely three hundred, mostly Cheyenne, surrendered to Miles at the Tongue River cantonment.

Fifty-one lodges of Minneconjou Sioux under Lame Deer refused to come in. Miles got word from surrendering Cheyennes that the Miniconjous were on the Rosebud, hunting buffalo and gathering edible plants. After receiving reinforcements in late spring of 1877, he set out to find them. The soldiers found the Indians on a tributary of the Rosebud on May 7. In the battle that followed, Lame Deer was killed and the Minneconjous fled. The camp was burned and most of the horse herd was slaughtered. Miles ordered some of the horses saved, and later used them to mount four companies of the Fifth Infantry. The scattered Indians were harried and pursued until they surrendered in the late summer.[66]

Several groups of Sioux remained on the Northern Plains, including Sitting Bull's people. An effective network of communication remained intact despite the fracturing of the confederacy. Messengers passed between the camps bringing news of reinforcement of the Fort Peck garrison in November, the soldiers' battle with the Sioux and Cheyenne on the headwaters of the Tongue River in February, and activities on the Missouri River reservations and among the Canadian tribes.[67] Sitting Bull had been considering escaping to Canada since the summer of 1876.

Just days after the battle of the Little Bighorn, a group of Sioux and Cheyenne headmen held a series of councils to decide what to do next. Sitting Bull argued that the American soldiers would harass the Indians relentlessly. Despite their victory, the Sioux would face a black and uncertain winter. "We have two ways to go now," he reportedly said, "to the land of the Grandmother, or to the land of the Spaniards."[68] Mexico was far away, although doubtless some southern-ranging Cheyennes knew that country was a haven for the Comanche and Kiowa. "Grandmother's Land," Victoria's British Dominion of Canada, was a couple of hundred miles to the north.

Canada had been a sanctuary in the past. Siouan tribes had hunted game and gathered edibles on that land for many genera-

---

[66] U.S. Secretary of War, *Annual Report, 1877*, "Report of Lieutenant-General P. H. Sheridan," 55–56.

[67] This network of information is not well defined. It was probably the result of a constant exchange of information among nomadic peoples, and contained much gossip and hearsay that was not always accurate. Colonel Miles and other army officers may have been able to tap into the network by employing Indians or white traders as "spies" for pay.

[68] Vestal, *Sitting Bull*, 182. According to Vestal, this quote is from interviews with Sioux Indians who either participated in these events or knew people who did.

tions, and fought with Canadian Indians for the right to do so. Early Siouan groups ranged through the woodlands and rocky Canadian Shield areas northwest of Lake Superior in the seventeenth century, when French and British trappers and missionaries first penetrated the area. Simultaneously, conflict and competition for food with the Chippewas and other tribes to the east had pushed many Sioux onto the plains. By the nineteenth century the Teton branch had moved west of the Missouri River. The Yankton branch lived north of this area. One Yankton tribe, the Assiniboines, ranged far into Canada, forming close ties with Cree Indians and other Canadian tribes.[69]

The Dakota Tetons of the 1870s were familiar with the Canadian prairies. Indians living on both sides of the border had freely mixed and made war for a long time. Most of the tribes maintained cordial relations with the British representatives from the Hudson's Bay Company, French-Canadian engagées, and the Métis—peoples of French and Indian descent who hunted and trapped on the Canadian plains. The Sioux often traded with these groups for arms, ammunition, and supplies.[70]

Sitting Bull believed that sanctuary could be found in Canada, but the others were not willing to leave their traditional ranges. The council could not reach a decision, and the tribes gradually broke apart on the march eastward from the Little Bighorn, each group intent upon avoiding the soldiers until spring allowed them to reunite.

Sitting Bull was still convinced that a flight to Canada was the best option. He rejected the idea of living on a reservation, and still believed that the whites would kill him in revenge for the battle at the Little Bighorn.[71] He was a political and religious leader first of all, and a warrior's death evidently did not appeal to him. But escaping to Canada posed a number of problems. The most serious was the hostility between the Teton Sioux and some of the Canadian Indians,

---

[69] See Owen J. Dorsey, "Migrations of the Siouan Indians," *American Naturalist* 20 (March 1886). Also, Robert H. Lowie, *Indians of the Plains* (New York City: Greenwood, 1954).

[70] This trade can be documented by the reports of the agents of the Fort Peck and Fort Belknap agencies in the Annual Reports of the Commissioners of Indian Affairs for 1876 and the years before; also in the reports of the North-West Mounted Police in National Archives of Canada, Record Group 7, "Records of the Governor-General's Office," File 2001, vol. 3; also in the Fort Benton *Record*, 1873–1876, and in the *Manitoba Daily Free Press* of Winnipeg, 1875–1876; also by reports of various officers in the Annual Reports of the Secretaries of War, 1876–1877. In the 1850s, however, the Sioux often conducted raids against the Métis. See W. L. Morton, "The Battle of Grand Coteau, 13–14 July 1851," *Manitoba Scientific and Historical Society Papers*, series 3, no. 16 (1961): 37–41.

[71] Vestal, *Sitting Bull*, 182–83.

especially the powerful Blackfoot tribes, the Crees, and the Canadian Chippewas. Sanctuary would be difficult to find if the intrusion of large numbers of refugees ignited a competitive war for territory and food. A way needed to be found to moderate relations with the Canadian tribes, halt the fracturing of Sioux unity, and meet the growing strength of the American soldiers on the Northern Plains.

All of these concerns might be met by forming an alliance between the tribes of the Northern Plains, north and south of the border. The idea may have had great appeal for Sitting Bull, who understood that external threats could forge bonds between peoples with disparate interests. What better threat could serve than the growing power of white men? Such an alliance might mean that the Sioux exile in Canada would be temporary, since a unified front would more than balance the power of the American army and the Dominion of Canada's North-West Mounted Police. Success in battle would attract more Indians to the cause, thereby halting the erosion of Native American resistance on the plains. Sitting Bull appeared to believe that a confederacy of Indians on both sides of the border would push the whites back into the East.[72]

It was an appealing idea, although not an original nor a historically successful one. The Sioux acted quickly during the month after the Little Bighorn battle. Messengers from Sitting Bull rode across the plains, reportedly bringing to each tribal group a rifle cartridge and a piece of tobacco—a choice between war and peace—and an invitation to send representatives to a council near the Cypress Hills on the southwestern Canadian plains. In July, emissaries of the American Sioux met with leaders of a number of Canadian tribes, including the Santee and Yankton Sioux, Assiniboines, Blackfeet, Crees, and Gros Ventres at a site near Frenchman's Creek. Especially supportive of the Sioux plan were the Santees and Yanktons, who called white men "dogs and cowards" and predicted that all whites would soon die.[73]

Other tribes were not as sanguine about the proposed confederacy. The Yanktonnais, Gros Ventres, Chippewas, and others expressed little sympathy, and resisted repeated efforts by Sitting Bull's representatives to give a commitment to the alliance. Many of the Canadian Indians had little reason to join: the few whites they

---

[72] The newspapers in Montana manifested great anxiety over such an alliance; see, for example, "News From the Front," *New North-West*, 25 August 1876. These speculations were not confined to the Americans; Canadians in Winnipeg also engaged in alarmist predictions.

[73] U.S. Commissioner of Indian Affairs, *Annual Report, 1876*, "Report of John S. Wood, U.S. Indian Agent, Blackfoot Agency, Montana," 490.

knew lived at Fort Macleod and Fort Walsh, and scattered settlements and posts. The land still seemed large enough.[74]

The key to the coalition were the Blackfeet—the powerful Bloods, Piegans, and Blackfoot tribes that straddled the border in a region stretching from the Cypress Hills to the eastern ramparts of the Rockies. The Sioux could not convince the Blackfeet on either side of the border to ally themselves against whites. Headmen at the Blackfeet Agency on the upper Marias River told the Indian agent there that "the Sioux were their enemies, and they would fight them if they ever came into this country, and the whites were their friends, and they would help them whip the Sioux."[75] In fact, the meetings between the Blackfeet and the Sioux worsened relations between them. For a period immediately following the council, war threatened between the American Blackfeet and the Canadian Santees and Yanktons who had taken Sitting Bull's offer so seriously. The Santees and Yanktons believed that the Blackfeet were fair game for raids and intimidation since they had rejected the plan.

The Canadian Blackfeet were equally as negative. Although the Sioux offered them a large portion of the spoils, they pointedly announced their loyalty to the North-West Mounted Police. The Sioux then modified their proposal and sought an alliance only against American whites, but the Blackfeet rejected that suggestion as well. Nor were the Crees or other Canadian tribes convinced. One source in the Mounted Police predicted that if the American Sioux tried to cross the border, five thousand Canadian Indians would drive them back.[76] The effort to form a pan-Indian movement on the Northern Plains had failed.

Sioux representatives continued to offer inducements to other tribes throughout the rest of the year, but their success was limited.[77] The effort was severely hampered by the onset of winter and the constant harassment by Miles's soldiers. During the winter and spring of 1877, Sitting Bull's people, moving constantly to avoid the soldiers, heard how the army had run down other groups in the Yellowstone and Powder River regions. When he appeared in Crazy

[74] Ibid., "Report of Thomas J. Mitchell, U.S. Indian Agent, Fort Peck Agency, Montana," 495.

[75] Ibid., "Report of John S. Wood, Blackfoot Agency," 490.

[76] "The Proposed Alliance With Canadian Indians for War on the American Whites," *New York Times*, 20 September 1876. This article quotes a letter from S. E. Denny of the North-West Mounted Police to the headquarters staffs of the Department of the Missouri and the Department of the Platte.

[77] "Loyalty of the North West Tribes," *Manitoba Daily Free Press*, 31 July 1876.

Horse's camp a few days after the battle with the Tongue River soldiers, Sitting Bull reportedly tried to save what was left of the confederacy by urging the Indians to join him in an exodus across the border. There they could recover and regroup until they were strong enough to return and fight the Americans again. But his arguments were rejected.[78]

In February of 1877, Sitting Bull's camp was hit once more by elements of the Fifth and Twenty-Second Infantries, with Miles commanding. Casualties were light on both sides, but lodges and stores were burned again, and the Sioux were forced to retreat into the northern edge of the Big Dry. Destitute once more, many Indians believed that a decision about their future had to be made quickly.[79]

In the early spring, word arrived of Spotted Tail's efforts to induce the Oglalas, Sans Arcs, and Miniconjous to return to the Missouri River reservations. The reports also suggested that Miles was trying to persuade the Indians to surrender at the Tongue River cantonment. As the weather warmed and more Indians straggled onto the reservations, those Sioux who refused to give up probably felt very frustrated. Unity had been fragmented, resistance had been crushed, and attempts to form an alliance with other tribes had yielded nothing but disappointment. Sitting Bull remained convinced that his people could not surrender without facing death or incarceration, but his presence in the United States was rapidly becoming untenable. Miles had not relaxed the pressure against the Indians north of the Tongue River cantonment; his patrols still marched out onto the Big Dry.

Sitting Bull probably knew that there were American Sioux already living in Canada by the winter of 1877. As early as August 1876, the *Benton Record* reported the presence of six hundred lodges near Fort Walsh. These may have been Yankton Sioux from the Fort Peck and Fort Belknap reservations, who often hunted buffalo across the border. In late September and mid-October, however, two letters from Fort Walsh to the *Benton Record* claimed that substantial numbers of American Indians were crossing the border, and making overtures to the Canadian tribes in the vicinity. A dispatch from the Mounted Police commander at Fort Walsh to the agents at Fort Peck and Fort Belknap warned that a large party of Sioux camping ten miles north of the border had planned to raid both reservations. The

[78] Utley, *Frontier Regulars*, 278. See also, U.S. Secretary of War, *Annual Report, 1877.* "Report of General N. A. Miles," 435.

[79] "Thrashing the Hostiles," *Helena Herald*, 7 February 1877. This article quotes dispatches from Miles to Gen. Alfred Terry.

raid never materialized.[80] Canadians in the Fort Walsh area reported that the Sioux began crossing into Canadian territory just after September 1. According to the Indians, they were driven north by Miles's and Terry's troops. By October an estimated twelve hundred were living in the Cypress Hills.[81]

Throughout the winter small groups of Sioux crossed into Canada, usually along Frenchman's Creek. Some tried to buy arms and ammunition from traders at Fort Walsh, but they were turned down because the Mounted Police believed the weapons might be used on raids into Montana.[82] The number of refugees increased dramatically in December, when the small camps of Teton Sioux were swelled by Yanktons and Santees. One Santee headman, Inkpudu, or Red Paint, claimed to have killed Custer's brother Thomas at the Little Bighorn. Now, he told the Mounted Police, the Sioux were all "subjects to the Queen."[83]

Sitting Bull's people also tried to buy ammunition from Fort Walsh when none could be found at Fort Peck. They were turned down, but soon found another source. The Canadian Métis traders had no misgivings about selling arms to American Indians, and they were probably the Sioux's major supplier during the winter and spring. Good relations with the Métis gave Sitting Bull two advantages: the Sioux gained important links to a large and influential Canadian frontier group, and Sitting Bull bought surplus ammunition to distribute among other camps besides his own. Forced to rely on the headman's connections, other bands and groups accorded him a valuable amount of respect. Sitting Bull, through frequent trips among the camps, consolidated his position as the principal leader among those Sioux north of the Yellowstone River.[84]

By April, the federation of Sioux south of the Yellowstone River had shattered. Crazy Horse remained at large, but most of his people had deserted him and returned to the reservations. He was a fugitive on the run, a fate that probably caused Sitting Bull some anxiety. Crazy Horse's Cheyenne allies, who had been nearly destroyed by Col. Ranald Mackenzie's troops on the Powder River, surrendered and were sent to Indian Territory. Small groups in

[80] "War News," *Benton Record*, 29 September 1876. Also, "Correspondence: Cypress," *Benton Record*, 20 October 1876.

[81] "Sioux Refugees," *Manitoba Daily Free Press*, 11 October 1876.

[82] "Our Fort Walsh Letter," *Benton Record*, 26 November 1876.

[83] Ibid., 22 December 1876.

[84] U.S. Secretary of War, *Annual Report, 1877*. "Report of the General of the Army," 411.

northern Wyoming still held out, but Miles and his Tongue River soldiers were reportedly gearing up for another push against them.

With most of the remaining Sioux either across the border or close by with Sitting Bull, there was no one left to appeal to, no more Indians to gather together. The nine months since that bright day on the banks of the Little Bighorn had been filled with failure and disaster. Sitting Bull could only try to avoid the fates of Dull Knife or Crazy Horse—to be "sent away" or hunted down in an empty land. At least he might retain some power, if not over an alliance of Indians, at least over his own life and the lives of a small number of his people living in freedom and exile. He may even have maintained hopes of building a confederation of Canadian tribes.

During the last days of April, Sitting Bull received news of more troops arriving at the Tongue River cantonment from the east. On May 1, word came that Miles and his soldiers were moving—where was not clear. A detachment of the Seventh Infantry from Fort Shaw in western Montana was also in the field. Sitting Bull decided there was no point in waiting any further. On May 7, Superintendent James M. Walsh of the North-West Mounted Police at Fort Walsh learned that 130 lodges of Sioux had crossed the international boundary and were camped on Frenchman's Creek, seventy miles away. Sitting Bull was with them. Walsh had been expecting this development for months.[85]

During the winter and spring the superintendent had met with almost every group that crossed into Canada—Hunkpapas, Sans Arcs, Miniconjous, Two Kettles, even Oglalas. To each he lectured about Canadian law, and warned that the Northwest Territories must not be used as a haven from which to raid into Montana. He had recently returned from such a meeting in the Cypress Hills area, with Four Horns and Medicine Bear of the Teton and Yankton Sioux. Now the man who Walsh believed to be the leader of the remaining nonreservation Sioux had finally come over. On May 8, the superintendent and five police officers set out to find him.[86]

Learning that Miles had actually left the cantonment to find Lame Deer's Miniconjous only reinforced Sitting Bull's resolve to seek exile in Canada. Messengers arriving at the headman's camp on Frenchman's Creek told of Lame Deer's death and how the survivors had scattered, destitute and without shelter. Safe from the United States Army, the exiled Sioux would have to deal with the Mounted Police.

[85] "Our Cypress Letter," *Benton Record*, 11 May 1877. The *Benton Record* refers to Frenchman's Creek as the "White Mud River."

[86] Ibid. See also, National Archives of Canada, Record Group 7, Records of the Governor-General's Office, File 2001, vol. 3, pt. 3a, "Irvine to Scott," 6 June 1877.

CHAPTER 2

*"In another world, white men,
but different from any
I ever saw before . . ."*

*THE SIOUX SEEK ASYLUM IN THE
NORTHWEST TERRITORIES,
WINTER 1877*

The arrival of the Sioux refugees in the Northwest Territories in the winter and spring of 1877 evoked little surprise in Canada or in London. Months before, the reports of the Mounted Police and the editorial pages of a number of Canadian newspapers had predicted that the Indians would cross the border. In the spring of 1876, officers in the Northwest Territories corresponded with officials of the Canadian Interior Department on the possibility that harassed Sioux and Cheyennes would be forced across the border by American military operations in the Powder River and Yellowstone River regions. Dominion officials recognized the close relations between the Sioux and their Canadian counterparts. During the Minnesota war of the early 1860s, groups of Santee Sioux were forced across the border into the Fort Garry area by militia units and the U.S. Army. Many of them still lived in Canada in 1876.

Recalling the Minnesota case, a Canadian Interior Department official warned the assistant commissioner of the Mounted Police in

May 1876 that bands of Sioux would probably try to find sanctuary from U.S. troops in the Northwest Territories. Once there, they might use Canadian territory as a base for raids into the United States, thereby endangering relations between the two countries. The official predicted that the refugees would enter the Dominion somewhere south of Wood Mountain, a timbered area of hills and ravines east of Frenchman's Creek.[1]

British officials also manifested interest in the Sioux war. In the spring of 1876, Edward Thornton, the British minister at the Legation in Washington, D.C., passed along relevant information to the Foreign Ministry in London. To the foreign minister, the Earl of Derby, Thornton sent a copy of the Fort Laramie treaties of 1868 along with several covering letters explaining how the present war was simply the latest example of American capriciousness in their relations with the Indians. He seemed to be making a point about the reliability of negotiations and agreements with the United States.[2]

News of events on the Little Bighorn in June brought the war to the attention of a wider audience in Great Britain, including Parliament. Standing in the House of Commons in mid-July 1876, Sir William Watkins questioned the Undersecretary of the Colonial Department, James Lowther, about the situation in Montana. After noting that the war began with an American breach of a treaty, Watkins claimed that many of the Sioux were British subjects by virtue of their affiliations with Canada, and asked Lowther if the war was likely to spill over into the Northwest Territories. Were that the case, Watkins asked if the British government would intercede on behalf of the Sioux. Lowther replied that the British government had no information on the matter, and would not in any way interfere with the domestic affairs of the United States.[3]

The *New York Times* published an account of Watkins's remarks under the headline: "HAW!" The newspaper drew a loose comparison between the characters of Sitting Bull and "John Bull": "Neither has travelled much. Both have a certain amount of contempt for other people than themselves, which comes from seclusion and ignorance of the world outside." Should the Sioux "escape across the Canadian border," the *Times* continued, "we must assume that they would be as safe as Winslow or Tweed or any other thief." The Brit-

[1] National Archives of Canada, Record Group 7, Records of the Governor-General's Office, vol. 318, file 2001, pt. 3d; "Richardson to Irvine," 26 May 1876.

[2] Ibid., "Thornton to the Earl of Derby," n.d., probably spring 1876.

[3] Ibid., pt. 3a, "Memorandum," n.d.; also "Friends for Sitting Bull," *New York Times*, 24 July 1876.

ish, the newspaper hinted, would provide asylum for any enemy of the United States under the aegis of political dissent.[4]

The Canadian press, especially territorial newspapers, were less sure about granting the Sioux asylum and were careful to differentiate their position from those of Watkins and other British politicians. The *Manitoba Daily Free Press* in Winnipeg worried that while settlers in the Northwest Territories would be safe from the refugee bands because the Indians would not dare violate the terms of sanctuary, "the difficulties most to be feared from their unwelcome accession to our population would be of an international character; by which our present amicable relations with the United States might be jeopardized."[5]

This anxiety reflected the often tumultuous relations between the United States, Great Britain, and Canada. Coexistence in North America created a curious triangular relationship, often upset by competition and crisis. Over the years, American attitudes shifted from belligerence and annexationist sentiment to studied amicability, depending upon internal political circumstances and the state of relations with Great Britain. The British, on the other hand, possessed the responsibilities and problems of an empire, and policy toward the United States often manifested conservatism and bureaucratic turpitude. Authorities in London usually avoided confrontation, unless there was something to be gained by it. Between America and the Empire was Canada, an outpost of British culture with political ties to Great Britain and economic ties to the United States.

The Dominion's difficulties were worsened by several factors. First, British and Canadian interests and objectives had diverged since the creation of the federation. While British authorities pursued imperial policies and great-power competition in Europe, the Dominion government was more concerned with internal development and external trade. The enormous regional influence of the United States often caused Canadian issues and British policy to collide over economic and political matters, as British authorities attempted to smooth relations with the United States after 1865.

Second, recent events had exacerbated antipathy in the United States toward Great Britain and, by association, Canada. During the Civil War, southern "cotton diplomacy" and a series of imbroglios including the Trent and Alabama affairs had destroyed British credibility in America. Canada was not immune to these deteriorating

---

[4] "Friends for Sitting Bull," *New York Times*, 24 July 1876.
[5] "Dominion Forces in the North-West," *Manitoba Daily Free Press*, 17 July 1876.

relations: a raid on Saint Albans, Vermont, by Confederate sympathizers in Quebec angered many Americans. The intense sentiments against Great Britain moved Charles Dickens to write:

> If the Americans don't embroil us in war before long it will not be their fault. What with their swagger and bombast, what with their claims of indemnification, what with Ireland and Fenianism, and what with Canada, I have strong apprehensions.

Third, among Irish immigrants in the United States during the antebellum period were a militant nationalist group known as the Fenians. Dedicated to freeing Ireland from British rule, they conceived of a plan to create an Irish state in North America. Canada was their target. Operating out of bases in the United States, they sabotaged public works and offices, and laid siege to towns in New Brunswick, Quebec, and Ontario. The raids never amounted to serious threat, but Canadian-American relations suffered, especially after the U.S. government declined to act against the Fenians.

More serious was a fourth factor: the rekindling of opportunism and expansionism in the United States after the Civil War. Manifest Destiny may have been dormant during the war, but in the decades that followed industrialization and beckoning Pacific markets reignited territorial and economic ambitions. Attention turned toward Canada, as an editorial in the *New York Herald* pointed out in the final months of the war:

> When the termination of our civil conflicts shall have arrived, it may be the turn of our foreign enemies. . . . Four hundred thousand thoroughly disciplined troops will ask no better occupation than to destroy the last vestiges of British rule on the American continent, and annex Canada to the United States.[6]

Annexationist sentiment in America in the 1860s and 1870s was centered in Minnesota and Montana, where the citizens were aware of the sparsely populated regions of the Northwest Territories on the other side of the border. American entrepreneurs operated in the Territories with little regard for Canadian law or international convention. Minnesotans trapped and hunted over the border, and even fomented revolutions and troubles with local Indians. North of western Montana, across the border from Fort Benton, Americans cornered the fur and implement trade with Canadian tribes, and built trading posts on the major rivers. When the Dominion government sent Col. A. Robertson-Ross to the area in 1872, he reported:

[6] Untitled editorial, *New York Herald*, 24 June 1864.

I was informed that a party of American smugglers and traders had established a trading post at the junction of the Bow and Belly Rivers, about . . . 60 miles on the Dominion side of the boundary line. This trading post they named Fort Hamilton, after a mercantile firm of Fort Benton, Montana, U.S.A., from whom it is said they obtain supplies. . . . They have for some time carried on an extensive trade with the Blackfeet Indians, supplying them with rifles, revolvers, goods of various kinds, whisky [*sic*] and other ardent spirits, in direct opposition to the laws of both the United States and the Dominion of Canada.

. . . .

It is stated on good authority that during the year 1871 eighty-eight of the Blackfeet Indians were murdered in drunken brawls among themselves produced by whisky [*sic*] and other spirits supplied to them by [American] traders. [When these traders were remonstrated] by the gentleman in charge of the Hudson's Bay Post at Edmonton, they coolly replied that they knew very well that what they were doing was contrary to laws of both countries, but as there was no force there to prevent them, they would do just as they pleased.[7]

The Canadian government organized a paramilitary police force, the North-West Mounted Police, and dispatched it to the Territories in the summer of 1874. They were charged with extending control over the Territories, by removing foreign influences and setting up a system of law and order among the Indian and Canadian populations. They began by dismantling the American trading networks and arresting Americans who did not cooperate, acts which created hostility and resentment in Montana.

No one better understood the vulnerability of the Canadian position than Dominion authorities in Ottawa. Canada was a hostage to the United States for the good conduct of the British Empire. Anglo-American relations were of inestimable importance to Canada—more important in many respects than to either Great Britain or the United States. Since Canada's position was somewhat precarious, its role inclined toward moderation and peacemaking. But the dangers inherent in peacemaking were manifold; the Dominion was often under pressure to sacrifice its own sovereignty, for British authorities seemed willing to sacrifice Canadian interests for larger, imperial issues. For these reasons, any set of circumstances likely to upset relations with the United States prompted great concern in Ottawa.

[7] A. L. Haydon, *The Riders of the Plains* (London: Andrew Melrose, 1910), 12–15.

When reports of large numbers of Sioux crossing the international boundary reached Fort Benton, Montana, in the fall of 1876, however, reactions were relatively mild. The Mounted Police were anxious to cooperate with American authorities, and in late September James Walsh warned that a sizable party of Indians in the Territories was planning a raid on the agencies at the Fort Peck and Fort Belknap reservations. Although the raid did not materialize, Americans were impressed with Canadian efforts to cooperate. Another display of "good will" occurred in November, when, according to the *Benton Record,* American Sioux showed up at Fort Walsh and tried to buy ammunition. The Mounted Police quickly stopped this trade, prompting the newspaper's "Our Fort Walsh Letter" to speculate, "The Canadian authorities evidently have no desire to be drawn into complications with the U.S. government on this or kindred subjects, and the orders issued to the Mounted Police are in unison with that . . . as the sympathies of both officers and men are with the white population of Montana."[8] By the spring of 1877, the *Benton Record,* putting aside earlier charges that Canada afforded asylum to any "red cut-throat," confidently predicted that the Mounted Police would not allow the Sioux to find sanctuary in the Northwest Territories.[9]

The Mounted Police had a better grip on reality. They could do little to keep the Sioux from crossing in the Northwest Territories. To close the border would have required an armed force many times the size of police contingents in the region. Commissioner James Macleod, with tacit approval from the authorities in Ottawa, opted for a more moderate course. The Sioux would be told that they must obey Canadian law and not use the Territories to stage raids against the United States, or they would lose their status as refugees.

This approach was not as naive as it might appear. The Mounted Police believed that only a small number of Sioux would stay in the Northwest Territories, and that most would soon return to the United States, to surrender or resist the army on the Montana plains. During the Minnesota war in 1862, the Canadians had lacked the resources to repel Santee Sioux refugees, but most of those Indians had returned to the United States and those that had remained lived peaceably. It was unlikely, Canadian officials believed, that Sioux seeking sanctuary in Canada would violate the terms of their asylum. They would realize that the Mounted Police and the Canadian government were their only protection against American soldiers who might follow

---

[8] "War News," *Benton Record,* 29 September 1876. See also U.S. Commissioner of Indian Affairs, *Annual Report, 1876.* "Report of U.S. Indian Agent at Fort Peck, MT.," 494.

[9] "Our Fort Walsh Letter," *Benton Record,* 26 November 1876.

them across the border. Their own fears would mandate cooperation with Canadian authorities.

As early as mid-August of 1876, Macleod received word that Sitting Bull was making plans to seek refuge across the border, and had sent what amounted to a pledge of good faith. The report was third-hand, but the source was highly recommended by Assistant Commissioner A. G. Irvine and Officer L. N. F. Crozier. Several weeks before, Gabriel Solomon, a Métis trader, met another Métis named Laframboise, who had just returned from the United States. Laframboise claimed that he had spent the spring in Sitting Bull's camp, and talked with the headman at length in late April, two months before the Little Bighorn. Sitting Bull asserted that he would never make war on the Canadians because he found himself surrounded by Americans, "like an island in the middle of the sea." He had only two ways to go, "one to the country of the Great Mother, the other to the Spaniards," and had not decided which direction to take. According to Laframboise, Sitting Bull sat in council every day to consider the question. But he assured the Métis visitor that "as soon as he put his foot across the line on the Canadian soil he would bury the hatchet."[10]

In the fall of 1876, relations between the Mounted Police and the small groups of Sioux already living in the Northwest Territories were not good. The Sioux stole horses from the Canadian Blackfeet, and the police rounded up assorted culprits and returned the stock throughout the fall. Traders from Fort Benton returned to sell whiskey, guns, and ammunition to the Indians, while their hometown newspaper railed about how easy it was for the Sioux to rearm and resupply themselves in Canada so they could kill more of "our American boys in blue."[11] Detachments of police were sent out to intercept the traders, but the Bentonites eluded them.[12]

Only a few American Sioux crossed the border in the summer and fall of 1876. Most of them spent several weeks at Fort Walsh trading with the small community of merchants—sometimes in the dead of night—and then returned to the United States. Their numbers increased in mid-December when the Fifth Infantry and other American units began their winter campaign in the Yellowstone River region. By the time Black Moon and forty-two lodges of Hunkpapa Sioux reached Wood Mountain, there was a sizable encampment

[10] N.A.C., RG 7, file 2001, pt. 3d, "L. N. Crozier to A.G. Irvine, enclosing Affidavit of Gabriel Solomon," 18 August 1876.

[11] National Archives and Records Administration, RG 393, Records of the United States Army Continental Commands, "Letters and Telegrams Received," District of Montana, 1876–1886, n.d., dispatches between Maj. Guido Ilges and James Walsh.

[12] N.A.C., RG 7, file 2001, pt. 3d, "Crozier to Irvine," 18 August 1876.

already there. James Walsh and a couple of policemen visited the camp a few days later and reported 109 lodges totaling 500 men, 1000 women, 1400 children, 3500 horses, and 30 retired Seventh Cavalry mules. A little way off stood 150 more lodges of Canadian Santee Sioux under White Eagle, some of the survivors of the Minnesota War and their descendants.

Walsh had come to discuss Canadian law with the Indians. At six o'clock in the evening, White Eagle, acting as "host," assembled most of the American Sioux headmen, including The Little Knife, Long Dog, Black Moon, and The Man Who Crawls. After the preliminary introductions, the police officer asked the Sioux why they had come to Canada. Their unanimous reply was that "they had been told by their grandfathers that they would find peace in the land of the British; their brothers, the Santees, had found it years ago, and they had followed them." Walsh wanted to know if they intended to return to the United States. The Indians answered no. He then explained "the Queen's law in the North-West Territories," and stressed that killing, stealing, poaching, and whiskey-trading were forbidden. "May the Queen have pity on us," one headman responded.

The Sioux assented to Walsh's demands, but argued that without a good supply of guns and ammunition for hunting, they would starve. Walsh agreed that this was probably so, and promised to make arrangements with local Canadian traders to provide the Indians with enough arms to feed themselves. Riding back to Fort Walsh, he detoured to find Jean LeGarre, a French-Canadian trader who moonlighted as a justice of the peace for the territories. LeGarre immediately set out for Wood Mountain, but he only had 2000 rounds of ammunition and a few muskets to trade.

In his report to A. G. Irvine, Walsh recommended that adequate supplies be procured quickly for the Sioux, since the food situation was critical and more Indians would undoubtedly cross the border. Walsh also reported that the buffalo herds in the region were changing their range habits and had become plentiful in the Wood Mountain area. He suggested that four constables be assigned to the vicinity of the Sioux camp to distribute supplies and ensure the Indians' cooperation.[13]

Families and small groups of Sioux arrived at the Wood Mountain camp through the winter of 1877. The season was extremely harsh and often the trails to the border or to Fort Walsh became impassable. Information from the region was scarce. In early March, Walsh received a report that a large number of Yankton Sioux under Black Horn and Medicine Bear were camped on Frenchman's Creek,

[13] Ibid., "Walsh to Macleod," 31 December 1876.

and fifty-seven lodges under the Teton headman Four Horns had just arrived at Wood Mountain. The Yanktons had hunted in the Territories since before the Mounted Police had arrived, and Walsh knew their headmen. But the Teton Sioux were strangers, and close allies of Sitting Bull. Again, Walsh set out with a handful of scouts and police officers to lecture on the law.

Four Horns answered Walsh's questions in the same manner as the others had before him. They came in search of sanctuary from the Americans, he stated, and they intended to stay. Four Horns told Walsh that the Tetons had moved up from the Powder River country in twenty-five days, harassed by American troops until they crossed the border. Medicine Bear said his people came from the vicinity of the Fort Peck Reservation, and expected three hundred lodges of reservation Indians to join them soon. Both headmen claimed to be British Indians. They said their people had lived in Canada until about 1810, and their fathers had told them they would always find safety there.

The similarities in the Indians' accounts suggested two possibilities to Walsh. The story might be a common concoction, devised during prior councils. Or perhaps the Sioux really did have a memory of roots in Canada. Walsh concluded that there was probably some truth in both possibilities. Again, he explained Canadian law, noting that murder, theft, and rape were serious offenses, and added that he would hold the headmen responsible for the behavior of their people. After Black Horn and Medicine Bear arrived in the Teton camp to vouch for the Mounted Police, Walsh left three officers at a temporary camp in a stand of timber twenty miles east of Wood Mountain, and returned to Fort Walsh.[14]

Two months passed, and information reaching Fort Walsh indicated that the refugee Sioux remained undisturbed in the vicinity of Wood Mountain. But in mid-May word arrived that another large group of Indians had crossed the border and were camped near Frenchman's Creek, by the west end of the mountain at Pinto Horse Butte. Sitting Bull was rumored to be in that camp. For the third time, James Walsh rode out to the mountain to explain the law. The traveling was pleasant this time, for it was late spring and only melting snow drifts remained on the ground. Four constables rode with Walsh, and two Métis guides, one of whom was Gabriel Solomon.

They found the newest camp in the shallow valley of Frenchman's Creek. Sitting Bull was there, and after preliminary

---

[14] N.A.C., RG7, file 2001, pt. 3d, "Walsh to Irvine," 15 March 1877. See also Glenbow Museum Archives, M3636, "Anonymous, letter to Cora [Walsh]," 21 May 1890, 10–19.

introductions, Walsh told him that he was in Canada and asked for a formal conference. A meeting was called in front of the headman's lodge. Sitting Bull wanted to know how he and his people might obtain ammunition; they had very little left after fighting the Americans for so long. Walsh remained noncommittal, and promised only that enough would be provided to hunt with. That answer did not satisfy the Sioux, who were deeply worried that the American soldiers would soon cross the border and attack the Indian encampments at Wood Mountain. Sitting Bull described his people's sufferings in the United States at length, and claimed that the Sioux were British Indians, and he had led them home.

Walsh assured Sitting Bull that the Mounted Police would never permit the U.S. Army to pursue the Indians onto Canadian territory. Following a familiar pattern, he then introduced them to Canadian law. After warning the headmen that the Mounted Police would hold them responsible for the behavior of their people, he emphasized that the Canadian government would not tolerate the use of the Northwest Territories as a sanctuary from which to raid across the border. If the Sioux broke this or any other law, they would be tried and imprisoned for their offenses, or forced to return to the United States. Walsh believed that Sitting Bull was sincere when "he replied that he had buried his arms on the American side of the line before crossing to the country of the White Mother, and in the future if he did anything wrong on the American side, he would not return to this country anymore." He had come to Canada, he told Walsh, "to show that he had not thrown this country away."[15]

Walsh's visit might have ended there, but as the conference broke up, three Assiniboines rode into the camp, trailing a string of horses that appeared to have been stolen from a Catholic priest living in the Cypress Hills. White Dog, one of the riders, refused to tell Walsh where the horses had come from. Encouraged by the presence of so many Indians, the Assiniboines began to taunt the police officers. Walsh ordered his men to disarm the three Indians.

Surprised, White Dog and his comrades did not resist. Walsh held out a pair of leg irons and demanded that White Dog cooperate or face arrest. The Sioux became greatly agitated. White Dog mumbled an inconclusive explanation, and Walsh was content to warn the Assiniboines against horse theft. White Dog had lost face in front of a large crowd, and as he walked away he turned and muttered that he would meet Walsh again soon. Walsh grew "red as a radish,"

[15] N.A.C., RG 7, file 2001, pt. 3d, "Irvine to R. W. Scott, Canadian Department of the Interior," 23 May 1877.

and offered the Assiniboine a choice—apologize or be imprisoned. White Dog apologized.[16]

Walsh's reprimand apparently had the desired effect, for the refugees expressed a strong desire to accommodate his demands. But the officer still mistrusted Sitting Bull. The headman was "revengeful," he wrote to his superiors, and would cross the border to raid if given the opportunity. The matter was not yet resolved, and there was no assurance that it would be. Walsh's report emphasized that the Mounted Police had little control over the camps at Wood Mountain.[17]

Sitting Bull was also apprehensive, not only about American soldiers operating so close to the border, but about the Police as well. "In another world, white men, but different than any I ever saw before," he reportedly told some friends, "bold and fearless they entered my camp. It is indeed a great change—yesterday fleeing from them and cursing them as I moved—today they plant their lodge by the side of mine and defy me. Have I fallen? Is my reign at an end?"[18]

In late May, Assistant Commissioner A. G. Irvine was vacationing in Fort Benton, the only sizable settlement within a few days' ride of Fort Macleod and Fort Walsh. When news arrived of Walsh's visit with Sitting Bull, Irvine immediately set out for Fort Walsh. Arriving at the fort several days later, he learned that Walsh was temporarily away. Six Sioux representatives from Sitting Bull's camp were waiting for his return. Irvine rode out to greet them, and introduced himself as Walsh's "chief." The Indians told him that the Sioux were holding three Americans at Wood Mountain until the Mounted Police could arrive. One of the Americans was a "Black Robe," a Catholic priest.

Walsh returned to the fort that evening. On the morning of May 29 he and Irvine, along with Sub-Inspectors E. Dalrymple Clark and J. B. Allan, and the six representatives set out for Sitting Bull's camp at "the Holes," 140 miles east of Fort Walsh. After two days of hard riding, they topped a crest on the prairie and counted 150 lodges of Sioux below; nearby were another hundred lodges of Yanktons.

Irvine was impressed:

I was particularly struck with Sitting Bull. He was a man of somewhat short stature, but with a pleasant face, a mouth showing great

---

[16] Ibid. See also Grant MacEwan, *Sitting Bull: The Years in Canada* (Edmonton, Alb.: Hurtig Publishers, 1973), 88–89; also Glenbow Museum Archives, "Anonymous, letter to Cora [Walsh]," 27–28.

[17] N.A.C., RG 7, file 2001, pt. 3d, "Irvine to Scott," 23 May 1877.

[18] Glenbow Museum Archives, "Anonymous, letter to Cora [Walsh]," 23–24.

determination, and a fine high forehead. When he smiled, as he often did, his face brightened up wonderfully. I should say he is a man of about forty-five years of age. The warriors who came with him are all men of immense height and very muscular.

Sitting Bull welcomed the officers, and told Irvine and Walsh that the priest and his two companions had followed the Indians across the border to persuade them to return to the United States and live on the reservations. The headman was furious with the Americans, and stated several times that he could not return because the U.S. Army would kill his people; he only came to Canada to find peace. If Walsh had not "taught him Canadian law," Sitting Bull claimed, he would have put the priest's two companions to death and ordered the priest bound and escorted back across the border.[19]

The priest was the Reverend Abbot Martin Marty from South Dakota, one of the more active Catholic missionaries working on the Missouri River reservations. He claimed his visit was "official," and he carried letters of introduction from the the Catholic Commissioner in Washington, D.C., and the U.S. Commissioner of Indian Affairs. The letters instructed Marty to find Sitting Bull and offer him terms for surrender, and convince him to return to the reservations. The abbot acted surprised to see the scarlet jackets of the Mounted Police and professed not to know he was in Canada.[20]

Marty's choice of companions for this mission was unfortunate. Johnny Brughierre was his scout, on leave from his position as Col. Nelson A. Miles's chief tracker—a fact that was known to the Sioux. The abbot's interpreter was Joseph Culbertson, a mixed-blood of Sioux ancestry whose reputation among the Indians was stained by alcoholism and duplicity. Irvine later wrote that by refusing to kill these two, Sitting Bull displayed some sincerity about wishing to obey Canadian law. Sparing the trio and sending his representatives to find Walsh may also have been a way for Sitting Bull to convince the Canadian authorities of his good intentions. Irvine's sympathies were won, but Walsh remained doubtful.

That evening, when Marty asked Sitting Bull if he would agree to take his people back to the reservations, the headman turned to

[19] N.A.C., RG 7, file 2001, pt. 3d, "Irvine to Scott," 6 June 1877. The following account in the text is from this document.

[20] Given scout Johnny Brughierre's familiarity with the region, this is difficult to accept. It is also likely that the Sioux told Marty where he was. The abbot's authority extended as far as that of U.S. Commissioner of Indian Affairs J. Q. Smith—to the Canadian border. It would have been embarrassing for U.S. authorities to explain an "official emissary" operating in the Northwest Territories without the permission of the Canadian government.

Irvine and asked, "Will the White Mother protect us if we remain here?"

Irvine answered in the affirmative, and Sitting Bull declared, "What should I return for? To have my horses and arms taken away? What have the Americans to give me? They have no land. I have come to remain with the White Mother's children." The assembled Sioux noisily agreed. Irvine and Walsh quickly proposed to postpone a council until the morning of the following day. Sitting Bull agreed, but at eleven o'clock that night he showed up at Irvine's tent, where for three hours he outlined the injustices that the Americans had dealt to his people and to himself. He swore that American troops on Sioux reservations were ordered to "kill all who talked." The police officer listened sympathetically.

On the morning of June 2, a second meeting convened with the police officers, the abbot and his companions, Sitting Bull and many of his people, and the headmen from the nearby Yankton camp in attendance. Sitting Bull opened with a formal statement:

> The Americans who came here asked me if I threw our land away. I told them God did not tell me to. Crazy Horse is still holding it. He is looking at me to see if it is still good here.

Sweet Bird, a Miniconjou, stood and berated the Americans for stealing the Black Hills from the Sioux. Spotted Eagle affirmed that the Sioux had come to Canada only to hunt and live in peace, and accused the Americans of deliberately burning the prairies south of the border so the Indians would starve. At this, the Sioux became agitated, and Irvine and Walsh recessed the conference until after lunch.

Late in the afternoon the participants met again and listened to a prayer by Pretty Bear, a Hunkpapa who was a Catholic. Irvine told Sitting Bull that Martin had only come to find out if the Sioux would return to the United States or stay in the Northwest Territories. Sitting Bull refused to consider returning. The Sioux could not go back, he stated, and explained at length about the suffering of his people, concluding that God had told him not to fight the Americans, but to go north and live in peace in Canada.

At that point, Marty committed a serious error. He insisted that he only came as a messenger of God to convince the Sioux to do the right thing, and now he wanted to know their decision. Sitting Bull may have felt threatened by Marty, for among the Sioux some had affiliations with reservation Catholicism. Now the abbot, either through ignorance or by design, challenged Sitting Bull's authority. Gesturing in a sweeping manner, Sitting Bull turned to Irvine and said:

God is looking at me now, and you know it. If he has a treaty to sign, no one can destroy it but by God's Will [a reference to the loss of the Black Hills]. God told me that if anyone came from the East, to eat with him just the same. It is no use. God made me leader of the people and that's why I'm following the buffalo. God told me, if you do anything wrong your people will be destroyed, and that's why I came here. I was afraid.

Turning back to the abbot, he said:

You told me you came as the messenger from God. What you told me is not good for me. Look up, you will see God. Look up, as I am looking. You came and told me, as God's messenger, what to do, but I don't believe it. I have nothing but my hands to fight the white man with. I don't believe the Americans ever saw God, and that is the reason they don't listen to me. You know, as the "messenger of God" that they tried to kill me. Why did you wait till half my people were killed before you came?

If his people returned to the United States, Sitting Bull said, the soldiers would kill them. Did the abbot want that to happen?

Flustered, Marty tried to shift the direction of the conversation, and committed another error: "I did not come here to give any advice at all; if you remain here it is all right; if you come to America, you will have to give up your arms and horses." But the night before, Sitting Bull had told A. G. Irvine that when the abbot arrived in the camp he had told the headman: "I come with the words of God. . . . I want you to live, that is why I came here, that is what God told me to come and tell you." The Indians listened as Martin related that "the English" did not want them in the Northwest Territories, and that they had better return before they starved or lost their reservations in the United States. He said, "Try to do as I tell you."

Sitting Bull faced the abbot and demanded, "The thing you told me is not here; tell me today what you said yesterday."

"I don't want you to come back," Marty replied, "but if you wish to come, I would try to make it as easy as possible."

"It is not the same as yesterday today what you said," argued Sitting Bull. "I have told the Chief here," pointing to Irvine, "what you told me yesterday."

Marty stood up and said, "After hearing all this talk and what these British officers say, I would think you were better off on British soil." And he strode away from the council. That ended the matter, and the police persuaded the Sioux to allow the Americans to depart.

Marty's observations evidently bothered Sitting Bull, who tried to get some assurances from Irvine that "the English" really did not mind if the Sioux lived peaceably in Canada. The assistant commissioner remained carefully neutral, for the abbot's comments were accurate—the Dominion authorities did want to be rid of the Sioux. Irvine hinted that the government was unlikely to offer any aid to the Indians should they choose to exile themselves permanently in the Northwest Territories.

There were several reasons why Canadian officials were reluctant to offer assistance to the Sioux, even to defuse a potentially troublesome situation. Ottawa's hold on the Territories was still tenuous; as yet there was no road from Winnipeg to Fort Walsh and transportation depended largely on the river and rail networks in the United States. Ever conscious of events south of the border, Canada did not want to appear to be cooperating with "hostile" Sioux. Complaints to that effect had already been voiced in a number of Montana and New York newspapers. Just as important were the effects the Sioux incursion might have on relations between the Dominion and the western tribes. As Irvine and Walsh listened to the arguments between Sitting Bull and Marty, a commission led by territorial Lt. Gov. David Laird and Commissioner James Macleod of the Mounted Police was negotiating with the Blackfeet, Crees, and other Indians. The commission was attempting to extinguish tribal titles to lands on the western plains, and to establish reserves where the Indians could live without interference from Canadian settlers.

The Sioux threatened those negotiations by upsetting the balance of power in the Northwest Territories. The Blackfeet and Crees were especially uneasy because they were traditional enemies of the Sioux, and the Sioux camps abutted their hunting ranges. A recent shift in the migratory patterns of the buffalo had carried the bulk of the herds into the Wood Mountain region. The Blackfeet and Crees could not exploit those herds without challenging the Sioux. Already the edible resources on their own lands were becoming scarce.

The Mounted Police could not alienate the Sioux and expect to maintain order on the frontier. But Canadian officials realized that aid to the Sioux would inflame the Canadian tribes and probably lead to trouble. A middle course was selected: the Sioux could remain in the Northwest Territories and have the protection of the Dominion as long as they were peaceable, but they would receive no help. It was hoped that this sort of benign discouragement might eventually persuade the Indians to return to the United States, where they would receive assistance. But this course presupposed that the U.S.

government would be cooperative after the Dominion had extended sanctuary to the Sioux.

In late May, James Macleod reported on the apprehensions of the Canadian tribes to the Deputy Minister of the Canadian Department of the Interior, Alexander MacKenzie. The Sioux, Macleod wrote:

> have not been on friendly terms with the Blackfeet or Crees for years back. The Blackfeet, I know, are anxious about the invasion of their country; they say that before our arrival they were always able to keep them out, but they now wish to be friends, so long as (the Sioux) keep away.[21]

Mackenzie passed the information along to Lord Dufferin, the Canadian governor-general and the Queen's appointed administrative head in Ottawa. Dufferin decided that the issue could lead to serious consequences. In an urgent dispatch to the Colonial Secretary in London, he described a massive invasion of western Canada by eight thousand Sioux warriors, heavily armed and extremely hostile. These Indians were "mortal enemies" of the Canadian Blackfeet, he reported, and the entire northwest district was about to erupt into a conflagration. Dufferin claimed that the only way to avoid a war was to compel the United States government to remove the Sioux and intern them on their reservations. Might the British Legation in Washington, D.C., be instructed to ask the U.S. authorities to take steps in that direction immediately?[22]

Dufferin's warning was a ploy to coerce the British government to open negotiations with the United States on the matter as quickly as possible. Dufferin was no fool. He was aware of how critical the good will of the Canadian tribes was to Ottawa's hold on western Canada, and he agreed with Interior Ministry officials who felt that the sooner the Sioux left Canada, the better. Exaggeration was one way of reaching that end.

The dispatch was only the latest in a series of moves by the governor-general to bring the matter of the Sioux exiles before the United States government. Two weeks before he alerted the Colonial Department to the situation in the Northwest Territories, Dufferin sent a note to Frederick R. Plunkett, the chargé d'affaires of the British Legation in Washington. With the British minister, Edward Thornton, on vacation in Great Britain, Plunkett was the Legation's ranking officer. Dufferin enclosed an advisory from the Privy Council of Canada in his note, admonishing Plunkett

[21] N.A.C., RG 7, file 2001, pt. 3d, "Macleod to Mackenzie," 30 May 1877.
[22] Ibid., "Dufferin to the Secretary of State for the Colonies," 18 June 1877.

to move the Government of the United States to take such steps as will induce these Indians and any others who may similarly cross the Boundary Line, to return. . . . Any delay in so important a matter may be attended with serious embarrassment to both the Governments of the United States and Canada.[23]

Plunkett predicted that negotiations between the two governments would be long and ultimately unsatisfactory, and he asked what the Canadian position would be in that event. He informed Dufferin that he had forwarded the Privy Council report to the Earl of Derby in the Foreign Ministry in London for further instructions, and indicated that he needed both permission and instructions before bringing the matter to the attention of the U.S. Department of State.[24]

The Earl of Derby thought the matter sufficiently important to telegraph Plunkett with instructions to honor Dufferin's request.[25] On June 23, Plunkett met with U.S. Secretary of State William Evarts and formally requested that the United States government take steps to induce the Sioux to return to their reservations.[26] Later the same day a note from Evarts was handed to Plunkett at the British Legation. Evarts had submitted the request to "the proper authorities," the Department of the Interior.[27]

There the matter rested for more than a month, until the Foreign Ministry in London, alarmed by Dufferin's prognosis for war in the Northwest Territories, prodded Plunkett to further emphasize the British government's concerns. On July 24, Plunkett presented himself at the State Department and found Evarts and the Deputy Secretary of State, F. W. Seward, waiting for him.

Plunkett began by asking about the status of the British and Canadian request, but Evarts blithely dismissed the question by stating that the matter had been referred to Secretary of the Interior Carl Schurz, and he had not yet responded. Instead, Evarts wanted to talk about the political and diplomatic status of the Sioux exiles. He told Plunkett that these Indians must be regarded as "political offenders seeking asylum in a foreign country" and that it would "be contrary to the treaties [with Great Britain] for the United States to demand their extradition." Canada could not tolerate American troops crossing the border to drive the Sioux back to the reservations, Evarts argued, nor could the North-West Mounted Police expel the Indians

---

[23] Ibid., pt. 3a, "Dufferin to Plunkett," 3 June 1877.
[24] Ibid., "Plunkett to Dufferin," 7 June 1877.
[25] Ibid., 20 June 1877.
[26] Ibid., 27 June 1877.
[27] Ibid., pt. 3d, "Evarts to Plunkett," 23 June 1877.

without the assistance of the British army. The situation, Evarts concluded, must remain as it was.

Plunkett, a little disconcerted, could not agree:

> I said that, as far as I could see, the matter was not so difficult of arrangement; all that was desired was, as far as I understood, that the United States Government would allow the Sioux Indians tolerably favourable terms on which to return.

He reminded the Secretary that Indians were of a different political status than that of white American citizens: they were wards of the federal government and had no political privileges. Evarts replied:

> The United States Government could not be expected to hold out great temptations to return, in the case of savages, whom they were only too happy to have got rid of, and who committed all sorts of crimes before quitting the United States. He could only think that if the United States troops ever caught hold of those among the savages who had robbed and murdered on American territory, before they crossed into Canada, they would probably shoot them.

Wrote Plunkett to the Earl of Derby:

> I contented myself with saying that I hoped he would consider the question carefully and dispassionately, for no matter how glad the United States might be to get rid of her troublesome Indians by forcing them onto Canadian territory, the gain would be more than counterbalanced by the danger of such a proceeding bringing on complications with Her Majesty's Government.

On that note, the meeting adjourned.[28]

Within a week, Evarts took the offensive. On July 31, Plunkett was handed a note from the secretary informing him that the President of the United States had just received a letter from the governor of Montana complaining that Canadian traders were selling guns and ammunition to American Blackfeet Indians. Apparently, when American traders had refused to sell the Indians arms pursuant to a recent presidential order, the Blackfeet simply crossed the border and purchased all they could in the Northwest Territories. "I have the honor," Evarts wrote, "to request that the matter be brought to the attention of the Canadian Government, which, I feel assured, would not wittingly countenance any acts which would increase the power of the Indians to indulge in their propensities for murder and plunder."[29] Evarts was using a dependable tactic: answer one complaint with

[28] Ibid., "Plunkett to the Earl of Derby," 24 July 1877.
[29] Ibid., "Evarts to Plunkett," 31 July 1877.

another and cloud the issue. Since by this time the Sioux were no longer a front-page issue in most American newspapers, Evarts was free to operate as he saw fit.

Most New York and Washington, D.C., papers failed to note Sitting Bull's escape into the Northwest Territories. On May 30, two weeks after the Sioux had crossed the border, the *New York Times* reported that the Indians' camp had been hit by four companies of the Second Cavalry and a mounted contingent of the Fifth Infantry south of the Yellowstone River. According to the *Times*, the camp was destroyed and fourteen Sioux were killed, including Sitting Bull. The article was mistaken: Colonel Miles had attacked a Cheyenne camp under the headman Lame Deer. On June 17, however, the *Times* reported that Sitting Bull was "thoroughly subdued" and living in Canada near Wood Mountain. The article described the meeting between the Sioux headman and Martin Marty, and reported that the abbot claimed he and Sitting Bull "agreed" it was best for the Sioux to remain in Canada. According to Marty, the war was over.[30]

Most newspapers in Montana paid more attention to the situation at Wood Mountain, except for the *New North-West* in Deer Lodge, which did not print the news of the Sioux exile in Canada until late July. The *Helena Herald* reported Marty's mission at the end of June, and James Walsh's interview with Sitting Bull in mid-July. As early as May 11, "Our Cypress Hills Letter" in the *Benton Record* stated that Sitting Bull and 130 lodges had crossed the border and were camped on Frenchman's Creek, and James Walsh and five men had gone to meet them. The *Record* printed a number of detailed reports on subsequent activities around Wood Mountain and at Fort Walsh, and criticized the confusion of facts and predictions in other newspapers. By July, when the diplomatic issues of the Sioux exile became apparent, eastern newspapers relied chiefly upon the Department of State and the Department of War for information.[31]

The Sioux exile stirred anti-British sentiment in the United States that summer. The *Helena Herald* reported that "the Canadian authorities look upon the United States horses, mules and arms [captured at the Little Bighorn] as spoils of war." Furthermore, the *Herald* decried the idea that "if Sitting Bull can be found, he will be killed or conquered, or probably driven again beyond the border [where he will find] refuge." The newspaper described the Mounted Police as "an

[30] "Severe Indian Fighting," *New York Times*, 30 May 1877; "Sitting Bull Thoroughly Subdued," ibid., 17 June 1877.

[31] "Sitting Bull Crosses the Line," *New North-West*, 20 July 1877; "Sitting Bull— Visit of Father Marty," *Helena Herald*, 30 June 1877, "Sitting Bull," 16 July 1877; "Our Cypress Hills Letter," *Benton Record*, 11 May 1877, "Fort Walsh," 15 June 1877, "Sitting Bull," 29 June 1877, "Sitting Bull," 16 July 1877.

army of observation," and hoped that Colonel Miles could lure Sitting Bull south of the Missouri River, where U.S. Army operations would be "safe from foreign complications," and "exterminate the savages."[32]

Comments in the *New York Times* also reflected an anti-British sentiment. After reporting in late June that there were no high-level government communications between the United States and Great Britain concerning the Sioux refugees, the *Times* concluded that nothing in international law or in applicable treaties between the two nations prevented "either voluntary expatriation or emigration, especially for begging purposes." But two weeks later the *Times* reported that the Sioux had conducted raids into Montana to break the monotony of exile, and that the British or Canadian governments had done little to stop them. The British would "howl in anguish" if Miles pursued the Indians across the border into Canada as Col. Ranald Mackenzie had pursued the Kickapoos into Mexico a few years before. The *Times* described the Mexicans as "a sharp race of brigands" who did not mind the intrusion, but the British were "spoiled" and "soft," and did not understand how Americans dealt with Indians.[33]

The *Benton Record* took exception, praising the Canadians and criticizing United States Indian policy:

> In what disgraceful contrast appears the agency system of the United States when compared to the just, humane and economical policy adopted by the Canadian government. By a simple code of laws administered by a handful of incorruptible men, the very self-same Indians that here on American soil will not be controlled, are not only prevented from plundering and murdering defenseless whites, but made to respect the people whose laws they dare not disobey. . . . We are reliably informed that the negotiations regarding Sitting Bull now pending between the United States and Canada, are likely to result in an entire change of policy on the part of our own Government. The transfer of the Indian Bureau to the War Department is the one contemplated, we hope.[34]

The frequent visits by the Mounted Police to Fort Benton had paid off.

In Winnipeg, the *Manitoba Daily Free Press* covered the situation on the Northern Plains extensively, for, like Fort Benton, the

[32] "Sitting Bull," *Helena Herald*, 16 July 1877, "The Hostiles West and North," 16 July 1877, "The Northern Boundary," 27 July 1877.

[33] "Sitting Bull's Flight to Canada," *New York Times*, 25 June 1877, "Fugitive Redskins," 7 July 1877.

[34] "The Indian Policy," *Benton Record*, 29 June 1877.

town's commercial and political communities had direct interests in the Northwest Territories. Unlike most Montana newspapers, the *Free Press* emphasized the effects the Sioux exile might have on relations between the United States and Canada. The editorial bias of the newspaper was generally anti-American and sympathetic toward the Indians.

The *Free Press* demonstrated this slant as early as August of 1876. Responding to criticisms in the *New York World* that the Sioux would be granted asylum in Canada "simply because they have dusky skins," the *Free Press* stated that if the Indians crossed into the Territories, it was because of an unjust war caused by a nation that dishonored its treaties. Under the circumstances, the Sioux were eligible for asylum. The *World* had challenged the Dominion government to arrest and deport the Sioux to face charges as "murderers and outlaws," but the *Free Press* replied that the Sioux "are no more liable to surrender by us than the Bosnia and Herzegounian refugees were liable to be given up by Austria to the tender mercies of the Turks." The *Free Press* claimed that Canada could govern "difficult" Indians and prevent them from raiding United States territory

> far more successfully . . . than the United States authorities prevented the Fenian raids on us, for the simple reasons that we would try in good faith. But preventing hostile raids is one thing; giving up political prisoners is another and very different thing.[35]

As for charges that the Mounted Police could not effectively control the Indians, the *Free Press* countered:

> If a powerful nation like the United States cannot control the movements of their own Indians, it would be absurd for them to blame the small force at the disposal of the Canadian government for failing to hold them in check.[36]

The *Free Press* did not receive news that the Sioux had sought sanctuary at Wood Mountain until other newspapers had reported it. In July 1877, after Sitting Bull's people had been living on Frenchman's Creek for two months, the *Free Press* published a story debunking a rumor that the Sioux headman had brought 2000 lodges into Canada. There were only 600 lodges affiliated with Sitting Bull, the newspaper assured its readers, in addition to 350 lodges of Santee refugees of the Minnesota War, 200 lodges of Teton Sioux under the headman Bear Spirit, and 127 lodges of "Dakota Sioux war

[35] "Sioux Refugees and Fenian Invaders," *Manitoba Daily Free Press*, 3 August 1876.
[36] "Sioux Refugees," ibid., 11 October 1876.

parties."[37] This estimate was still far too high; the Mounted Police reported several encampments numbering no more than 150 lodges apiece, but exaggeration was not unusual in newspaper reports that summer.

One person living in Winnipeg who read the *Free Press* avidly was United States consul James W. Taylor. A former annexationist from Minnesota, Taylor had decided that a career with the State Department might further his designs for the Northwest Territories. During the winter and spring of 1877, he visited frequently with hunters, traders, and Mounted Police officers returning from the plains. As a result, he learned about the movement of the Sioux into Canada before most of Winnipeg did. On March 8, he wrote a letter to J. L. Cadwalader, the Acting Secretary of State, and reported that a large group of Sioux had crossed the border near Wood Mountain, leading 1000 horses and mules captured from the U.S. Army. Taylor mistakenly reported that the camps of Four Horns and Medicine Bear were led by Sitting Bull and overestimated their number at five thousand, a thousand of whom were "warriors." He also observed that an alliance with twelve hundred Minnesota Sioux exiles in the region was possible, and warned Cadwalader that the Mounted Police would be unable to "restrain the Sioux refugees from making their present encampment a base for raids upon the posts and settlements of the Missouri River."[38]

The Department of State did not respond to Taylor's letter until late July, when Assistant Secretary F. W. Seward asked Taylor to characterize the situation at Wood Mountain. Taylor reviewed the entire affair, and characterized the attitudes of the Sioux refugees as surly and hostile. "The Indians seem determined to obtain ammunition at all hazards, and make no secret of their intentions to renew a campaign in the Yellowstone Valley," he wrote. "I hear of mules, branded U.S. [Army] which have been sold for ammunition. When traders refuse to exchange peacefully, the Indians resort to threats and violence." Taylor emphasized that the Mounted Police did not have the strength to control the Indians, and reported that four Canadian traders recently had been robbed by a party of twenty-seven Sioux.[39]

On the same day, Seward wrote to Taylor describing his and Secretary Evarts's meeting with the British chargé d'affaires. The letter from the United States consul in Winnipeg confirmed Evarts's

[37] "The Sioux Indians," ibid., 16 July 1877.
[38] N.A.R.A., Record Group 59, Records of the Department of State, file T–24 10–9–5, "Taylor to Cadwalader," 8 March 1877.
[39] Ibid., "Taylor to Seward," 24 July 1877.

belief that American interests would be better served if the Sioux remained in the Northwest Territories, but it also raised the disturbing possibility that the Canadian authorities could not restrain the Sioux from raiding into Montana. Taylor's statements that Canadian traders were selling ammunition to the Sioux—even at gunpoint—along with the complaints of the governor of Montana provided grounds for Evarts's protests to Plunkett on July 31.

Evarts's charges were not entirely unexpected at the British Legation, where assertive American diplomacy and the edgy personality of the secretary of state were well known. But the American position was likely to cause a furor in Ottawa, where Lord Dufferin and the Privy Council were not satisfied with the progress of negotiations. Again, the interests of Canada were sacrificed for imperial issues. In the context of Anglo-American relations, small groups of Indians causing trouble along a sparsely populated border were not worth sacrificing the delicate, post–Civil War rapprochement.

None of these matters found their way into the lodges of the refugee Sioux at Wood Mountain. During the summer of 1877 they hunted buffalo, restocked their food caches, and repaired shelters and equipment. The Sioux remained relatively stationary and avoided trouble. Their behavior was generally peaceable, although Sitting Bull continued his efforts to forge an alliance with other tribes. But they lived in fear, even though they knew nothing of the debate in Ottawa, London, and Washington. Mistrust of whites pervaded their councils, and the line of stone cairns that marked the mysterious boundary past which American soldiers could not go was only a day's march to the south. Wood Mountain was not a comforting place.

CHAPTER 3

"A Dangerous Precedent"

THE CANADIAN MINISTER OF THE INTERIOR VISITS WASHINGTON, D.C., SUMMER 1877

In late July 1877 the governor-general of Canada visited the United States on personal business. He left behind an unsettled state of affairs in Ottawa. The Prime Minister and his cabinet were pressing the Privy Council to implement direct negotiations with the U.S. government concerning the refugees at Wood Mountain. Lord Dufferin had seized the initiative by warning officials in London and at the British Legation in Washington about the dangers of allowing the Sioux to stay in Canada. But the talks had bogged down in a malaise of politics.[1]

Before he left for America, Dufferin and the Privy Council gave tacit approval to a radical course of action proposed by the cabinet. Traditionally, matters pertaining to foreign relations were taken up on behalf of the Dominion of Canada by the British Foreign Ministry. It was an unwieldy arrangement that required communications

[1] N.A.C. RG 7, file 2001, pt. 3a, "Dufferin to Plunkett," 23 October 1877.

between Canada and the United States to be routed through the London Foreign Office and the legations, so that the British might keep a measure of control over a diverse and far-flung empire. The Dominion government, long dissatisfied with the arrangement, now decided to circumvent normal diplomatic channels and send a high-ranking cabinet member to Washington, D.C., to deal directly with the United States government. He was David Mills, a mild-mannered but very determined career politician who, by virtue of a clever intellect, rose to become minister of the Department of the Interior, the agency responsible for relations with Indians of the Dominion.

Mills arrived in Washington, D.C., on the evening of August 7, 1877. The next morning he presented himself at the offices of the British Legation and asked for the chargé d'affaires. Frederick Plunkett was not in, and Mills decided to walk the short distance to his residence. Plunkett was not particularly happy to see the Canadian minister of the interior on his doorstep, unannounced, so early in the morning. He listened with growing incredulity as the minister explained his mission. Mills claimed to be authorized by the Canadian secretary of state in an informal capacity, "to present our views to the British Legation, and with the sanction of the Legation to the authorities at Washington with reference to Sitting Bull and other hostile Sioux." Mills assured Plunkett

> that I made no claim to having any representative character; that I had not sought authority to enter into any formal arrangement with the Government of the United States, with reference to Sitting Bull, but that I was of the opinion it was better that I should appear unofficially, simply indicating the views of the Canadian Government.[2]

Plunkett was slightly put out:

> This request put forward so unexpectedly, and without any previous consultation with this Legation, as to whether the visit of a Canadian Cabinet Minister to Washington on an official mission, was desirable or not caused me some embarrassment.[3]

Two things were clear to both men: Mills was interfering with the traditional prerogatives of the British Legation, and Plunkett was not entirely trusted by the Canadian government to present the Dominion's point of view.

To Plunkett's credit, he agreed to aid Mills, and in the end he proved to be invaluable. The two men returned to the Legation, where Plunkett showed the Minister the notes that had passed between the

[2] Ibid., Mills, "Report," 23 August 1877.
[3] Ibid., "Plunkett to W. B. Richards," 11 August 1877.

Legation and the Department of State on the issue. After a few hours of discussion, the British chargé d'affaires took Mills down to the State Department. Evarts was out, so Plunkett introduced the minister to the assistant secretary, F. W. Seward, and pointedly explained that Mills's visit to the American capital was in an informal capacity. According to Mills, Plunkett

> informed Mr. Seward that I was there for the purpose of stating informally the views of the Canadian Government with reference to Sitting Bull and was prepared to make suggestions as to the steps that might be taken by the United States Government to induce the Sioux to return.

Seward advised them that this was not the business of the State Department. He suggested that the matter concerned the Department of the Interior, and that perhaps Mills should meet with his American counterpart, Secretary Carl Schurz. Late in the afternoon, Plunkett and Mills made their way over to the offices of Interior. Schurz listened without comment as Mills outlined the purpose of his visit. When he finished, the secretary invited the two men to the White House, where they were introduced to President Rutherford B. Hayes. After a short conversation, Mills later reported, "it was appointed that on the following day I should see Mr. Secretary Schurz and the Undersecretary of the Interior, Mr. Smith."[4]

At nine-thirty on the morning of August 9, Mills presented himself at Schurz's office, where he found not only the secretary of the interior and his undersecretary but also Secretary of War George W. McCrary and President Hayes. For several hours the men discussed United States and Canadian Indian policies, and debated the issue of returning the Sioux to their American reservations.[5]

Earnest conversation on the Sioux began when

> Secretary Schurz observed that he did not well see how they could secure the return of Sitting Bull and his Band; that they had made war upon the United States; that they had retired under arms across the Canadian frontier; that they were political offenders, and their return could not well be demanded under the Treaty of Extradition; but as a hostile force, he thought we were under obligations to disarm them.

Mills replied that discussing the problem from Schurz's point of view would be difficult and unrealistic. Disarming the Sioux was tanta-

---

[4] Ibid., Mills, "Report," 23 August 1877.

[5] Ibid. The following account in the text of the conversation between the participants is from the same document.

mount to abandoning them to hunger and deprivation; they were hunters and would probably start a war rather than starve. It was doubtful the Mounted Police could disarm more than a thousand reluctant warriors. Another solution was required. Mills rebutted Schurz's characterization of the Sioux as political offenders who were not eligible for extradition under current treaties:

> The United States had entered into certain treaty stipulations with the Sioux; [they] had not dealt with them heretofore as an integral part of the population, but rather as a separate community; that, from the Indian point of view, the hostilities were begun by the United States. . . . America ought therefore to induce the Sioux to return to the reservations where the U.S. government might control them, and not allow them to remain in the hands of a foreign government.

This backhanded argument was designed to play upon underlying American desires for security, but Schurz conceded that the Canadian minister had a point. The secretary stipulated that the Sioux must surrender their horses and arms before returning to the reservations— in effect, he demanded an unconditional surrender to American authorities. If the Sioux refused these terms, Schurz asked Mills, would the Canadian government disarm them?

The Canadian government had promised the Indians enough guns and ammunition to survive, Mills firmly replied. Dominion authorities would not discriminate against the Sioux by disarming them, because other Canadian tribes were allowed arms for hunting. The minister reminded the Americans that disarming the Sioux would condemn them to starvation, and place them at the mercy of other Indians who opposed their presence in the Northwest Territories.

Mills brought up another point: there were reports of shortages of buffalo and game in the Territories, and the situation could only become worse as the Indians at Wood Mountain continued to hunt. The minister complained that, although the activities of the Canadian traders could be regulated, it was impossible for the Mounted Police to keep American traders from Fort Benton from providing the Sioux with whatever guns and ammunition they could pay for. Given the dwindling food resources and the virtually unlimited supply of weapons the Americans could sell, Mills thought it "highly probable" that at a future date the Sioux would return to the United States and renew hostilities. There was little that Dominion officials could do to prevent it. In Mills's opinion, the most practical solution was to convince the refugees to return to the reservations in America quickly, where they could be fed and supervised.

Continuing on the same theme, Mills stated that Canadian authorities would not disarm the Sioux because it would humiliate them, and likely lead to war. Instead, the minister proposed an altogether different solution: why not gain their "good will" and "obedience" by giving them better weapons and more ammunition to promote good relations. If this were done, Mills predicted, the Sioux would willingly return to the reservations with American representatives, convinced that American intentions were honorable. Mills reported:

> The President observed that as he understood my representation, I regarded firearms as the implements by which the Indians obtained their subsistence, and that my recommendation to them was to buy up Sitting Bull and the leaders of the Sioux.

"Yes," Mills replied, "by doing them justice." He reminded Hayes that the French had secured Pontiac's loyalty in the eighteenth century through similar methods, and that Canadian policy since the Treaty of Stanwyx had followed the example with consistent success. "Savages were pleased with showy dress and a little attention," Mills told the President, and the cost was negligible.

Secretary Schurz asked the minister: "But how do you keep your whites in order?" The "true origin of the Indian difficulties of the United States," Mills later wrote, "was indicated by [this] question." But before the minister could answer, Secretary McCrary offered his own explanation of the American dilemma: the army did not have the manpower to police the borders of the reservations. There followed a highly critical discussion of congressional appropriations for the military.

Mills proposed that a commission be sent to the Sioux to offer terms that would enable them to return to the reservations. The president and both secretaries finally agreed to the proposal, but again Hayes stipulated that the Indians must give up their horses and arms if they wanted to return to the United States. Mills warned that the commission would surely fail if it insisted on these conditions, but Hayes and Schurz replied that arms and horses would be of no use on the reservations because there was no game to be hunted there. Mills suggested that the commissioners be given some kind of "discretionary power" on this issue:

> The President observed that if the conditions suggested were offered the Sioux, and they really refused to accept them, the Commissioners might, at all events, go so far as to ascertain upon what terms and conditions they would be willing to return.[6]

The meeting ended with a definite, if informal, commitment by the United States government to send a commission to the Northwest

[6] Ibid. This ends the account of Mills, "Report."

Territories to offer the Sioux conditions by which they might peaceably return to their reservations. President Hayes also cautiously agreed to give the commissioners "discretionary powers" over the terms of peace. It was not an overwhelming diplomatic triumph for David Mills, but under the circumstances, alone and unannounced in Washington, D.C., he could hardly have hoped to achieve more. He returned to the British Legation where he gave Plunkett an account of the meeting. He left for Ottawa on the following day.

Plunkett was not soothed by the apparent success of Mills's mission. In a letter to the Canadian cabinet the day after the minister had left Washington, D.C., the British chargé d'affaires wrote, "I cannot but point out that I consider it would be a dangerous precedent, were I to allow his practically semi-official Mission to pass without comment." In the future, Plunkett demanded, the legation must be consulted on issues relating to affairs between the United States and Canada.[7]

Plunkett also sent a report and a complaint to the Foreign Ministry in London. The Earl of Carnarvon responded with a pointed— yet diplomatic—note of disapproval to Lord Dufferin and the Canadian Privy Council. Referring to Mills's visit, Carnarvon thought it probable that some progress had been achieved. However, he expressed his "concurrence in the soundness of the principle laid down by Mr. Plunkett [as] to the importance of adhering in all ordinary cases to those forms and procedures which have been recognized as convenient and desirable." Further,

> Lord Carnarvon desires it to be understood that he does not press his view from any feeling of dissatisfaction with Mr. Mills, or with the language which he seems to have held and which Lord Carnarvon thinks as far as can be judged was very judicious, nor does he lay stress upon it as a matter of mere diplomatic form or etiquette, but for the reasons that questions arising in Canada, may, and very frequently will, have a direct bearing upon the interests of other portions of Her Majesty's Dominions. He suggests therefore that looking to the Imperial considerations which are involved in this question that if at any time the Government of the Dominion deem it expedient for a Canadian Minister to confer in local matters with the United States authorities in Washington, Her Majesty's Legation should be previously consulted.[8]

The unity of the Empire rested upon "Imperial considerations," and Mills's visit to Washington threatened this order. The Dominion author-

---

[7] Ibid., "Plunkett to W. B. Richards," 11 August 1877.
[8] Ibid., "Dufferin to Plunkett," 23 October 1877.

ities probably expected such a reaction. To the Canadians, however, "imperial considerations" were considerably less important than the mere "local matters" that threatened to disrupt an entire territory and upset relations with a powerful neighbor.

Dufferin was only slightly apologetic, and chose to regard Carnarvon's reprimand as a matter of etiquette. In a letter to Plunkett in October 1877, he explained that he had been visiting the United States during Mills's representation, and no one else in the Privy Council or the Dominion government had the authority to officially inform the British legation of the minister's coming. The "existing" emergency justified Mills's mission, Dufferin claimed, but the Privy Council of Canada acquiesced to the Earl of Carnarvon's disapproval.[9]

Plunkett set out to ascertain what damage, if any, the Mills visit had had on Anglo-American relations. He found little to be concerned about. In response to his inquiry, F. W. Seward sent a copy of a report to Secretary McCrary from General Sherman. Sherman reported that Colonel Miles "is very anxious to go to the border with a sufficient force to demand of the British Agents, that these Indians, now reduced to absolute want, and almost devoid of ammunition, be surrendered to him as prisoners." The general observed that he and General Terry had consulted and agreed that Dominion authorities ought to either "adopt" the refugees or force them back across the border "before they recuperate and resupply." If the Sioux "use British Territory as a base of operations against us," Sherman warned, "the Act will surely be the equivalent to an act of hostility, which I am sure the English authorities do not intend."

Sherman agreed to the proposed commission, but recommended that it offer the refugees the same terms of surrender given to other Sioux. If the commission succeeded, an escort of troops could meet the returning Indians at the border. But if the Sioux remained in Canada, Sherman warned, the circumstances would deteriorate as they had along the Texas-Mexico border, where Indians had raided settlements in the United States and then escaped by crossing the Rio Grande. The U.S. Army had not been satisfied with the amount of cooperation given by the Mexican government, and Sherman hinted that the Mounted Police would do no better. In a parting shot against the Canadians, he wrote, "It must be on the theory of the great right of affording 'refuge' to distressed Indians that Sitting Bull and his Allies have been permitted even to remain near the border."[10]

In the meantime, David Mills had arrived in Ottawa, and was attempting to put together a cohesive policy in response to the

[9] Ibid.
[10] Ibid., "Plunkett to W. B. Richards," 15 August 1877.

commission's upcoming visit. In a letter to Mounted Police Commissioner James Macleod, written a week after he returned from Washington, D.C., the minister reiterated his belief that the source of the problem was American Indian policy:

> It is hardly doubted that the breaches of faith of which the United States Government have been guilty towards the Indians, the misconduct of their Indian agents, and the system of fraud they have practised upon the various tribes under their jurisdiction, and the trespassed adventurers, who have gone on the reserves against the wishes and despite the remonstrances of the Indians, account in a great degree for the difficulties which have occurred between white men and Indians in the neighbouring Republic.

Mills asked Macleod to collect information on U.S. violations of treaties and obligations with the Sioux. If "unreasonable demands" were made upon the Dominion by the U.S. government, Canadian authorities might then be able to point out that their difficulties with Indians "have been due to the misconduct of agents and the Washington authorities and their failure to observe their various treaty obligations." Finally, Mills outlined an official Canadian response toward the predicted American position:

> We claim no right to interfere with the domestic concerns of the United States; but when misgovernment of any portion of that population is notoriously such as to give rise to Civil war on our border, to force a portion of that population upon our territory, and to impose upon us additional expense, we certainly have the right to remonstrate.[11]

In Washington, officials of the Hayes administration were impressed by Sherman's approval of the commission, by continued pressure from the British legation, and by Hayes's commitment to Mills. They moved quickly to set up the commission, but the difficulties finding experienced and accredited individuals who were willing to serve became almost comical. All who were asked, according to the *National Republican,* "suddenly fell sick. . . . The bare mention of travelling a thousand or two miles, and paying one's own expenses [until reimbursed—perhaps—by Congressional appropriation], to wait on the Hon. Sitting Bull, seems to act as a nausea upon those invited to serve on the Commission."[12] Despite the general affliction, in a few weeks it was announced that General Terry and Gen. William

[11] Ibid., pt. 3d, "Mills to Macleod," 20 August 1877.
[12] "The Sitting Bull Epidemic," *National Republican,* 24 August 1877.

McNeil, a retired army officer who had some experience with Indians, would carry out the commission's responsibilities. Getting Terry had been easy—Sherman, invoking an army tradition, had volunteered his subordinate. Finding the second commissioner assumed the proportions of a public joke until McNeil submitted to pressure from Sherman, an old friend.

David Mills informed Macleod of the selection in a letter dated August 24, and pointedly sent a copy to the British Legation to be presented to the U.S. Department of State. The minister asked Macleod to furnish an escort for the commission as soon as it reached the border. "The Government," Mills concluded, "is most anxious that the United States Commissioners should succeed in inducing the hostile Sioux who have come into our territory to return to the United States." Should the Sioux remain in Canada, Mills continued, conflict between them and the Canadian plains tribes would be an inevitable result of dwindling food resources and territorial disputes. Avoiding such a conflagration could become "a very considerable expense to the Government of Canada." Further,

> It is not at all improbable that they may also be disposed to make hostile incursions into the United States, and in this way become a source of international trouble. These Indians while engaged in hostilities with the United States, were reported to be guilty of acts of such barbarous cruelty that, should they again return for the purpose of scalping women and children, their conduct could not fail to excite the indignation of the Government and people of the United States against this country.

Because of the serious nature of the situation, Mills instructed Macleod to use every device to ensure the success of the commission. As soon as he and David Laird completed negotiations with the Canadian Blackfeet, the commissioner should proceed to Fort Walsh and represent the Canadian government at the commission meetings. Mills proposed that the Mounted Police bring as much pressure to bear on the Sioux as was possible. He suggested that the Indians be informed that "should they go for any hostile purpose into United States territory, the Government of the United States may be permitted to follow them with their Army into Canadian Territory, and that in such an event, they must not look for the friendship or protection of the Canadian Government."[13]

Mills's letter to Macleod was probably written as much for the edification of American officials as for the Mounted Police. In no instance would Ottawa or London accept the presence of the U.S.

[13] N.A.C., RG 7, file 2001, pt. 3a, "Mills to Macleod," 24 August 1877.

Army in the Northwest Territories. Such an incursion would establish dangerous precedents for the Canadian West or other areas of the British Commonwealth subject to American influence. Mills's suggestion that Macleod inform the Sioux that American troops might follow miscreant raiders across the border was meant to serve the dual purpose of pacifying the Indians and reassuring the U.S. government about Canadian motivations.

The minister of the interior played a mercenary game. He voiced concern to the President of the United States about the plight of a group of destitute, homeless human beings, and pointed accusingly at the government and the American people for breaking treaties and dishonoring obligations to their native populations. He also weighed probabilities, predicted eventualities, and suggested rather ruthless solutions. Mills tried eloquently to persuade American officials that they could best serve the interests of the United States by offering to return the Sioux to their reservations, where their needs could be met and they could be controlled. Then he ordered subordinates to collect information about the atrocities committed against the Indians to use against the United States in negotiations. He characterized the same Indians whose plight he had described so graphically as murderous savages who could be bought off with a few baubles. The minister intended to get rid of the Sioux by whatever means was possible.

The political status of the Sioux refugees confounded both American and Canadian officials, perhaps because the legal position of Indians in the United States was not yet clearly defined. During his first meeting with Plunkett, Secretary Evarts had characterized the Sioux as "political offenders seeking asylum in a foreign nation," and had stated that the treaties of criminal extradition did not allow the United States to request their return. Plunkett had reminded Evarts that Sioux Indians were "wards" of the Federal government and had no political position.

During his meeting with Mills, Carl Schurz observed that the Sioux "had made war upon the United States, [and had] retired under arms across the Canadian frontier, [and] were political offenders, and their return could not well be demanded under the Treaty of Extradition." At the time, Mills had replied that the United States "had not dealt with [the Sioux] heretofore as an integral part of the population, but rather as a separate community." But in his letter to James Macleod in late August, Mills chose to regard the Sioux as a part of the peoples of the United States. He wrote that "misgovernment of any portion of the [U.S.] population" would give rise to "a Civil war on our border," and force "a portion of that population upon our territory."

American officials considered the refugees as dissidents who had rebelled against the United States and afterward sought sanctuary with a foreign power. They were not eligible for criminal extradition. Yet these same officials often characterized the Sioux as murderers, criminals, and savages. British and Canadian officials also chose to characterize the Indians as whatever best suited their policy—as "wards of the Federal Government," a "separate community," or an "integral portion of the [U.S.] population."

Any of the definitions could be rationalized, given the contradictory status of Indians in the United States. The Supreme Court had defined Indians in the collective as "resembling a ward to that of his guardian," and as separate nations that were

> considered, by foreign nations as well as by ourselves, as being completely under the sovereignty and dominion of the United States that any attempt to acquire their lands or to form a political connection with them would be regarded as an invasion of our territory and an act of hostility.[14]

Under this interpretation treaties were effected between the United States and various tribes. In 1871, however, Congress suspended further treaties and instructed various committees and federal agencies to review those already in force.

Throughout the 1870s, the government was pressured to reform Indian policy, and one of the proposed changes involved clarifying the legal status of Indians. The Office of Indian Affairs recognized merit in this reform. In 1874, Commissioner Edward P. Smith described the situation as "anomalous" and observed that the status of Indians could not be ascertained as long as tribal affiliations remained in force. United States law did not extend to Indians, Smith concluded, and there was no legal provision by which an Indian could become a citizen. Smith's successor, John Q. Smith, agreed. He found no clear provisions for legal jurisdiction over Indians in 1876, and complained that "Indian affairs have heretofore been managed largely by the application of mere temporary expedients in a fragmentary and disjointed manner."[15]

Several proposals to clarify the status of Indians were brought before Congress during this period, but none had been acted upon as of the summer of 1877. The Supreme Court addressed the issue tangentially in October 1876, when Associate Justice Samuel F. Miller, writing for the majority, held that "sedentary peoples" who had been

---

[14]"Cherokee Nation v. Georgia," *United States Reporter* 30–1, 17–5.

[15]Francis P. Prucha, ed., *Documents of United States Indian Policy* (Lincoln: University of Nebraska Press, 1975), 144, 147.

accorded the rights and responsibilities of political affiliation previous to territorial acquisition by the United States came under the jurisdiction of the law. But nomadic, semi-independent tribes were not subject to the law as usually constituted.[16]

The Sioux refugees in the Northwest Territories were left in a peculiar position. Commissioner Edward P. Smith's assessment remained in force: their status was anomalous. Under the circumstances, Secretary Schurz's declaration that the Indians were political offenders seeking to escape justice in Canada made as little or as much sense as any other interpretation. Sioux resistance to the United States government might just as easily be characterized as a defense of property and lives against an aggressor nation; an argument which could have followed from the abrogation of the 1868 Fort Laramie Treaty guaranteeing the Black Hills as a Sioux Reserve. Extradition laws were useless in the existing situation. The issue devolved upon which nation was responsible for the Sioux refugees, and what could be done about them. The commission was a compromise.

Frederick Plunkett threw the resources of the British legation behind the commission proposal, sensing that Mills's agreement with Hayes was indeed progress. But as time passed he became concerned that the Americans were dallying unnecessarily, and he expressed his impatience to Secretary Schurz in late August. Schurz explained that the delay had been caused by difficulties in finding qualified people who were willing to serve. The two men who were finally selected, McNeil and Terry, would be held up for another week until official instructions could be issued. Also, Terry was ill, and no one knew when he would be ready to travel.[17]

The trip would be difficult for the commissioners, Schurz told Plunkett. The time required to travel from Washington to Fort Walsh would depend upon the level of water in the upper Missouri River. If travel by steamboat were still possible by early September, the commission could move quickly. If passage was prevented, an overland journey would delay the commission's arrival significantly. Schurz suggested that the Canadian authorities might best occupy themselves by arranging for a strong escort to meet the commissioners at a designated location.

The secretary then changed the subject. He believed that the commission would ultimately fail. The Sioux would not accept the terms of surrender the United States could offer, and even if they did they would hesitate to return with the winter season so near. The approach of bad weather would persuade them to turn down any

---

[16]"United States v. Joseph," *United States Reporter* 94, 614, 615.
[17]N.A.C., RG 7, file 2001, pt. 3a, "Plunkett to W.B. Richards," 25 August 1877.

offer, no matter how generous. Schurz had his own solution. He asked the astounded Plunkett if

> the simplest thing would not be for the Canadian Government to move "Sitting Bull" and his band somewhere to the North, away from the American frontier, for the Canadians could easily absorb them, as was shown by what they had done with the Sioux who went over in 1862.

Plunkett left Schurz's office convinced that American officials were trying to force the Canadian government to accept final responsibility for the Sioux. He visited the office of the Department of State and demanded to see Secretary Evarts. The secretary was out of town, but Plunkett obtained an appointment with Acting Secretary F. W. Seward the following evening. After describing his conversation with Schurz, Plunkett protested "against any unnecessary procrastination" in sending the commission to Canada. "I said I noticed a desire in this Country to throw on to the Canadian authorities all the onus of taking care of those Refugees," Plunkett reported, "and preventing their doing any more harm to the United States Troops."

Plunkett told Seward that it was impossible for three hundred Mounted Policemen to disarm the Sioux and keep them in Canada, or to prevent American traders from supplying them with arms and ammunition. The situation was critical, but to Plunkett "it seemed there would still be plenty of time to come to an arrangement, if the United States Authorities would be a little more expeditious in their preparations." He reminded Seward that he had asked the State Department to report on progress several times, and had waited for two months without a reply. During this period the United States would have no right to redress the Canadian government for damage done by Sioux raids.

Seward disagreed. Canadian authorities had allowed the Sioux to buy arms and ammunition, he said. Plunkett argued that the sales were approved for hunting purposes only. Seward then backed down a little and reassured Plunkett that the United States government was cognizant of the situation and agreed that the most satisfactory course was to return the Sioux to their reservations. Seward claimed that the delay in sending the commission involved finding appropriate people to serve, and obtaining funds to finance it.

Plunkett interrupted: "I was under the impression that the State Department had a Miscellaneous Appropriation for unforeseen events."

"Only in regard to Diplomatic Missions," answered Seward. The Sitting Bull Commission did not fall within the normal range of diplomatic operations, he explained. The State Department merely offered aid to the Office of Indian Affairs in the matter.

Plunkett "pointed out to Mr. Seward that, although the commission was to be sent by the Indian Bureau, and was therefore technically not a Diplomatic one, its object was to reconcile the conflicting interest of two nations, and therefore, practically it ought to be treated as Diplomatic, and paid for as such."

Seward tried to reassure the British diplomat that Congress would eventually defray all of the commission's expenditures. In the meantime, he added, the commissioners would have to meet the costs out of their own pockets.

"Things look unpromising," Plunkett wrote that night.

The situation looked even less promising the next day, when word arrived that William McNeil had suddenly taken ill and was unable to travel. Gen. A. G. Walker was to take his place, but later Plunkett learned that Walker had declined to serve.[18]

That evening, Plunkett sat in his office writing to the Canadian government :

> I regret to have to add that I notice at the State Department a decided feeling that they have nothing to say to a private arrangement with another Department; and I cannot help thinking that, if the arrangement had been come to through the ordinary channels of communication between the two Countries, some of the difficulties now arising might have been avoided.

As he closed his report, Plunkett was handed a note from Seward. There were no further developments concerning the commission, wrote the Acting Secretary of State. Plunkett would have to consult with the Secretary of the Interior if he wished to pursue the matter.[19]

Even as Plunkett sat in his office bemoaning the United States government's lack of cooperation, an event was taking place that would drastically affect the stalled commission's chances for success, and add a new element of tension to the difficult situation in the Northwest Territories. Far in the west, a large group of Nez Perce Indians were fleeing across Yellowstone National Park, eluding soldiers and sweeping up parties of tourists in a desperate attempt to reach the lands of their former allies, the Crows. Victims of a misunderstanding over territorial boundaries set by a treaty they never signed, the Nez Perce were seeking sanctuary from the U.S. Army, just as the Sioux had before them. They knew about the refugees in Canada. If the Crows would not help them, Joseph, Looking Glass, Poker Joe, and the other Nez Perce headmen planned to take their people across the border to Wood Mountain.

[18] Ibid. This portion of Plunkett's letter was written the following day.
[19] Ibid.

CHAPTER 4

"You Belong on the Other Side;
This Side Belongs to Us"

The flight of the Nez Perces began as a result of a misunderstanding over the territorial claims of certain groups along the Wallowa River in Oregon and near the mouth of the Salmon River in Idaho. In 1863, the United States government negotiated a treaty establishing the Lapwai reservation on the Clearwater River in Idaho, but neglected to include the traditional ranges of the Nez Perces. Proposals to modify the situation in the early 1870s did not meet with the approval of these Indians, and when American officials threatened to use the army to force them onto the reservation, violence erupted. On June 12, 1877, while the Canadian governor-general requested that the British Legation bring the matter of the Sioux refugees to the attention of the United States government, a party of Nez Perces murdered several whites in the Salmon River area. Fearful of the reaction to these killings, many of the nontreaty Nez Perces fled to the east to escape the army. At first they sought refuge in Montana, but a bloody battle with Col. John Gibbon's Seventh Infantry on the Big Hole River convinced them that safety could only be found with their former friends, the Crows.

The flight of the Nez Perces was highly publicized, not only in the United States, but in Canada, Great Britain, and in other European nations. The appeal of their cause and the ability they demonstrated as they escaped or mauled superior American forces generated public sympathy, especially in the eastern United States. As the Nez Perces swung through Yellowstone National Park and headed to the north across the plains, they discovered that many of the Crows were employed by the U.S. Army as scouts. After beating off repeated attacks by soldiers and their Indian allies, the Nez Perce headmen determined to find a haven with the Sioux in Canada.

The decision was not unexpected. The *Benton Record* reported on August 10 that a Nez Perce woman on the "Kamiah" Prairie in Idaho claimed Chief Joseph told her that he was taking his people to join Sitting Bull in Manitoba. In late July and again in August, the *Helena Herald* claimed that Sitting Bull and "1300 warriors" were on the south side of the border, tearing down the boundary markers and riding as far as the Musselshell River, "waiting patiently" for something to happen. The Sioux refugees seemed to expect the Nez Perces at any time, the *New York Times* reported. The *Manitoba Daily Free Press* expressed anxiety over Sitting Bull's alleged attempts to forge an alliance between the Plains Indians on both sides of the border. To many commentators, the Nez Perces' flight toward the border indicated a general uprising on the northern Plains.[1]

Augmenting this fear was the sudden disappearance of the Sioux refugees from their accustomed camping sites near Wood Mountain. For several weeks the Mounted Police searched for the Indians without success. In the meantime, a series of dispatches from Colonel Miles was forwarded from the Department of the Dakota headquarters in Saint Paul to the State Department in Washington. Miles reported that his scouts had spotted thirteen hundred Sioux warriors on the American side of the border, a story that eventually found its way into the *Helena Herald*.[2] The colonel was prone to exaggerate and his information on this occasion was mistaken, but the dispatches were generally accepted.

[1] "Joseph Going to Meet Sitting Bull," *Benton Record*, 10 August 1877; "The Northern Boundary Line," *Helena Herald*, 27 July 1877; "Sitting Bull Scorns Peace," *New York Times*, 25 September 1877; "The Storm in the Northwest," *Manitoba Daily Free Press*, 13 September 1877.

[2] N.A.R.A., RG 393, District of the Yellowstone, Letters and Telegrams Sent, 1876–1881, "Miles to Adjutant-General, Department of the Dakota," 30 June 1877. See also U.S. Secretary of War, *Annual Report, 1877*, "Report of the General of the Army," "Report of Colonel N. A. Miles," 68–75.

A month later Miles wrote to department headquarters reporting that James Walsh and Sitting Bull had had a falling out, and the police officer had ordered the Sioux to leave the Northwest Territories. The Indians were camped on the Milk River in U.S. territory, Miles claimed, and they were preparing to move south into the Big Dry where he and his troops had campaigned against them the year before. In a letter to the various regimental officers stationed on the Tongue River, Lt. George Baird, Miles's adjutant, predicted that the Sioux and the Nez Perces would join forces somewhere on the Yellowstone River, after which they would establish a secure stronghold in the Big Dry. Miles's strategy, Baird wrote, would be to interpose his troops between the two groups and prevent them from finding one another. Baird notified the officers that they had authority to chase the Sioux as far south as the Wind River Range in Wyoming.[3]

After reading Miles's dispatches, Acting Secretary of State F. W. Seward sent for Frederick Plunkett. Here was an answer to the British diplomat's questions about the proposed commission. Delays in sending the commission were inevitable, Seward said, until it could be discovered where the refugees were. Plunkett was surprised. Would it be possible, he asked, to issue two sets of instructions to the commission, one if the Sioux were found in Canada and another if they had returned to the United States? Then the commissioners could leave for the border immediately. Seward promised to consult with the secretaries of war and the interior, and asked what sort of escort the Canadians could provide and where it would meet the commission. He wanted assurances that this escort would be strong enough to guard against Sioux "treachery." Plunkett, in turn, promised to consult with his superiors.[4]

By August, the Mounted Police still had not found the Sioux, but they did not believe Colonel Miles's reports.[5] Eventually, when rumor after rumor of Sioux movements south of the border proved unfounded, the United States government agreed. Late that month, Seward and Plunkett met again to discuss the commission, and the acting secretary reported that there had been no further sightings of the Indians in Montana.[6] Rather than wait any longer, the Hayes administration was prepared to dispatch General Terry and his secretary, Capt. H. C. Corbin, to Saint Paul with two sets of instructions.

---

[3] N.A.R.A., RG 393, District of the Yellowstone, 1876–1881, Letters and Telegrams Received, "Miles to Headquarters," 19 August 1877.

[4] N.A.C., RG 7, file 2001, pt. 3a "Plunkett to W. B. Richards," 30 August 1877.

[5] Ibid., "W. B. Richards to Plunkett," 29 August 1877.

[6] The Indians Miles identified as the refugees were later determined to be hunters from the nearby Fort Belknap and Fort Peck reservations.

If Terry found the Sioux in the Northwest Territories, he would offer terms of peace. If the Sioux had returned to the United States, he would personally direct military operations against them. Furthermore, an acquaintance of Terry's in Saint Paul with limited diplomatic experience in South America might be willing to serve as a second commissioner. If Terry could not convince him to go, the general would proceed as the sole acting commissioner.[7]

The next day a detachment of Mounted Police located the Sioux encampment on the Canadian side of the border, only a few miles from Wood Mountain.[8] But the news was not reassuring. The Nez Perce were still moving north, and on September 1 they emerged from the Absaroka Mountains and started across the Montana plains. The commission would be traveling across the region to which the Indians seemed to be heading, and there was speculation that Chief Joseph would join Sitting Bull at about the same time Terry and his entourage arrived at Fort Walsh. What that might mean, given the small number of Mounted Police in the Northwest Territories, was the subject of some anxiety among American officials.

Another problem arose over the specific instructions that were issued to the commission. David Mills had maintained that the terms of surrender should be equitable—simply an agreement to cease hostilities and return to the reservations. President Hayes had reluctantly agreed, but later Sherman had recommended that the terms be limited to unconditional surrender. Terry held the same view, and when the Hayes administration began to discuss the instructions for the commission, the suggestion that it have "discretionary powers" was dropped.

The commission's chances for success were thought to be slight, largely because of the inflexible terms it could offer, and the expected response of the refugees. As the time for Terry's departure drew near, the general opinion seemed to be that the United States government was simply going through the motions for the sake of Anglo-American relations. The *National Republican* saw no point in sending a commission:

> We hope . . . that the talk about a treaty with Sitting Bull will be abandoned. Such a policy may be well enough for the Canadian Government, but our relations to the Indians are quite different. It will not do for us to humiliate ourselves by treating with a chief who has twice defeated us. We must subdue him by main force.[9]

[7] N.A.C., RG 7, file 2001, pt. 3a, "Plunkett to W.B. Richards," 1 September 1877.

[8] Ibid., "William Buckingham to Mr. Kidd," 5 September 1877.

[9] "Treating With Sitting Bull," *National Republican*, 30 August 1877.

According to the *New York Times*, the Dominion government had asked that the Sioux be given complete amnesty. The newspaper rejected such a policy, and suggested that the Indians be allowed to return only after they were "stripped. Otherwise, this distinguished band of exiles can amuse themselves on British soil." The *New York Tribune* did not want to accept responsibility for the Sioux: "These Indians were not driven into British Territory, but retreated there voluntarily, and, of course, for their conduct the United States cannot be responsible." The *New York Herald* saw no chance at all for the commission's success. It was expected to fail, reported the *Herald*, because the Sioux would not surrender. Dominion authorities were powerless to control the Sioux, and U.S. Commissioner of Indian Affairs John Q. Smith had predicted that they would renew the war in the Yellowstone River area in the summer of 1878, once they were rearmed and resupplied by Canadian traders. To the editor of the *Benton Record*, the signs indicated war. The Montana newspaper reported that the Sioux were firing the prairie north of the Marias River. The Blackfeet would join them soon, and the Nez Perces were rapidly moving toward the Canadian border. "Everything appears at the present moment to favor a universal outbreak. . . . It is very necessary that the entire county be warned of the impending danger."[10]

Into this maelstrom of rumors and confusion the commission would be sent. A second commissioner had been found: A. G. Lawrence, a retired army general who had served as a U.S. minister in Central America. He had no experience on the western frontier and knew little about the Sioux, but he possessed a respectable reputation and, more important, he was willing to serve. On the 6th of September, the commission received its "official" instructions from Secretary of War George McCrary and Secretary of the Interior Carl Schurz. They were "directed by the President through the War and Interior Departments" to carry out various tasks:

> It is the object of your mission, undertaken at the suggestion of the Government of the Dominion, to ascertain what danger there may be of hostile incursions on the part of Sitting Bull and the bands under his command upon the territory of the United States, and, if possible, to effect such arrangements, not unacceptable to the Government of the Dominion, as may be the best calculated to avert that danger. To this end you will put yourself in communication with Sit-

---

[10] "Our Canadian Neighbours," *New York Times*, 10 August 1877; "Action in Regard to Sitting Bull," *New York Tribune*, 6 September 1877; "The Troublesome Sitting Bull," *New York Herald*, 10 August 1877; "The Storm Brewing," *Benton Record*, 24 August 1877.

ting Bull in such manner as, under existing circumstances, may seem to you most judicious.

Severe restrictions were placed upon the discretionary powers of the commission:

> According to all recognized principles of international law, every government is bound to protect the territory of a neighbouring friendly state against acts of armed hostility on the part of the refugees who, for their protection from pursuit, have crossed the frontier. While the Government of Great Britain will be most mindful of this obligation, the President recognizes the difficulties which, in dealing with a savage population, may attend to its fulfillment, and he is, therefore, willing to do all in his power to prevent any interruption of the relations of good neighbourhood, and to avert a disturbance of the peace of the border, even to the extent of entering into communication with an Indian chief who occupies the position of a fugitive enemy and criminal.
>
> You are, therefore, instructed, in the name of the President, to inform Sitting Bull and other chiefs of the bands of Indians recently escaped into the British possessions, that they will be permitted peaceably to return to the United States and occupy such reservations as may be assigned to them, and that they will be treated in as friendly a spirit as were other hostile Indians who, after having been engaged with Sitting Bull and his followers in hostilities against the United States, surrendered to our military forces. This treatment, however, can be accorded only on condition that Sitting Bull and all members of the Indian bands who take advantage of this offer of pardon and protection . . . [surrender] all their firearms and ammunition, as well as all their horses and ponies. . . . You will insist upon this condition to its full extent, and not make any promises beyond that of a pardon for the act of hostility committed as stated above.

Nowhere in the instructions was there a mention of discretionary powers granted to the commission if the Sioux refused to unconditionally surrender. In fact, if the Indians did decline their offer, the commissioners' instructions were explicit:

> In case the Indians refuse to return to the United States upon such terms, you will then break off all communication with them, and the Government of Great Britain will, no doubt, take such measures as may be necessary to protect the territory of the United States against hostile invasion.[11]

[11] U.S. Commissioner of Indian Affairs, *Annual Report, 1877*, "Report of the Commission Appointed by the President of the United States Under Instructions of

The instructions probably doomed the commission to failure even before it left for Fort Walsh. The Hayes administration did not intend to let the Sioux return across the border except under terms that would allow the United States government complete control over their lives.

The real designs of the Hayes administration were revealed in the references to the responsibilities of Great Britain. It was the "obligation" of British authorities to safeguard American lives and property "against acts of armed hostility on the part of refugees who, for their protection from pursuit, have crossed the frontier." The United States government would allow the Sioux to return only under strict terms of surrender, as a gesture of goodwill to Canada and Great Britain. But it was unlikely that the refugees would accept these terms, and the British and Canadian governments would then be forced to "take such measures as may be necessary to protect the territory of the United States against hostile invasion." Earlier, Secretary Schurz had proposed that the Canadian Government "move 'Sitting Bull' and his band somewhere to the North, away from the American frontier . . . for the Canadians could easily absorb them." If the commission failed, the Sioux would become Canada's problem, and the United States government would be rid of a large number of Indians it considered to be "troublesome."

On September 8, two days after receiving the instructions, Terry and his secretary left by railroad for Saint Paul, where they were to meet with General Lawrence. On the same day F. W. Seward informed Frederick Plunkett of their departure. Plunkett wired the news to Ottawa, observing that if the commissioners failed to convince the Sioux to return, Canada would have to deal with the Indians in whatever way it could.[12]

Terry and Corbin arrived in Saint Paul on September 11, and met with Lawrence the next day at the headquarters of the Department of the Dakota. The two men agreed to hire Jay Stone, an interpreter. They also agreed that the commission's instructions ought to be changed in one minor aspect. Both felt that it was absurd to dismount the Sioux at the border should they decide to surrender. Disarming the Indians was enough; they could be dehorsed on the reservations. The commissioners telegraphed Secretary McCrary to request the change.[13]

the Honorables Secretary of War and Secretary of Interior to Meet with the Sioux Chief Sitting Bull," 719.

[12] N.A.C., RG 7, File 2001, pt. 3a, "Plunkett to W. B. Richards," 8 September 1877.

[13] U.S. Commissioner of Indian Affairs, *Annual Report, 1877*, "Report of the Commission . . . ," 719–21.

Terry also telegraphed Lord Dufferin in Ottawa outlining the commission's timetable. He noted that the commission would use the well-traveled wagon road between Fort Benton and Fort Walsh, and requested an escort to meet them at the border on September 29. One other matter needed attention. Terry had ordered Colonel Miles to provide three companies of the Second Cavalry to escort the commissioners from Fort Benton to the border. But Miles would need these troops if he were required to pursue and engage the Nez Perces, so Terry mailed orders to Col. John Gibbon, commander of the District of Montana at Fort Shaw, to provide the escort instead.[14]

Getting to the border turned out to be an adventure. After leaving on the morning of September 13, the commissioners made good time, traveling first to Omaha, and then on the Union Pacific railroad as far as Pocatello Junction in Idaho. Arriving there on September 16, they found a message waiting for them: President Hayes had agreed to modify the commission's instructions regarding the Sioux's horses. On September 17, the commission took a stagecoach to Helena, where they procured horses from the local army garrison and rode north to Fort Shaw. They reached the fort on September 25, ahead of the mail from Saint Paul. Colonel Gibbon had no idea they were coming. An escort was difficult to arrange, since the Seventh Infantry had been mauled by Nez Perces at the battle of the Big Hole.[15]

Gibbon called up a company of the Seventh Cavalry from Fort Ellis, but the soldiers did not arrive until October 4. Already six days late, Terry and Lawrence started for Fort Benton that evening. Arriving in town at noon on October 6, the commissioners learned of discouraging news. The local garrison commander, Maj. Guido Ilges, had intercepted the Nez Perces north of Cow Island on the Missouri River, and had retreated after a brief skirmish. A civilian volunteer from Fort Benton had been killed, and the town was in an uproar.[16]

At midnight, a courier rode into Fort Benton with news that Colonel Miles and mounted elements of the Fifth Infantry, along with the Second and Seventh Cavalry, had intercepted the Nez Perces on the northern flank of the Bear Paw Mountains, forty miles south of the Canadian border. Convinced that the Indians were moving to join the Sioux, Miles had quickly led his command north and west from the Tongue River cantonment to interpose the force between

[14] Ibid., 721–22.

[15] Ibid., 722. Gibbon and his command had been shot up in a pitched battle with the Nez Perces at the Big Hole barely a month before.

[16] Alvin Josephy, *The Nez Perce Indians and the Opening of the Northwest* (New Haven: Yale University Press, 1965), 593–94.

the Nez Perces and Wood Mountain. The courier brought alarming reports that messengers from the Nez Perces had gotten through to the Sioux before the soldiers surrounded their encampment at Bear Paw. Miles expected his northern perimeter to be assaulted soon by more than a thousand warriors led by Sitting Bull. The colonel anxiously called for supplies and reinforcements.[17] Terry decided to send the commission's escort and their supply wagons to the Bear Paw battlefield immediately, and they left the next morning. He and Lawrence would stay in Fort Benton until the Nez Perces surrendered or the intentions of the Sioux exiles became clear.[18]

Miles's position was tenuous. Several Nez Perce riders had eluded the ring of troops and were already in the vicinity of Wood Mountain. When scouts reported the location of the Nez Perce camp on September 30, the colonel worried that the Indians might escape again or, worse, wait for reinforcements from the Sioux. Miles ordered an immediate frontal assault, but the Nez Perces shattered it with a withering fire that inflicted heavy casualties. The soldiers managed to scatter the horse herd and strand the Indians, enabling Miles to order a fall-back and a siege. He ordered another assault the following day, but it also failed.

For six days, the troops encircled the Nez Perce at the Bear Paws, and Miles grew anxious. Not only might he have the Sioux to contend with, but units under Gen. Oliver O. Howard, who had trailed the Nez Perces since June, were hastening up from the south. Unwilling to share credit for a victory with Howard, Miles tried different methods to force the Indians to give up, including taking Joseph prisoner under a white flag of negotiation. Nothing worked. The Nez Perces, hoping for relief from the Sioux, continued to hold out through a series of severe blizzards.[19]

The same snowstorms hit the encampments at Wood Mountain where Sitting Bull and other Sioux headmen were considering a course of action. Scouts and escaping Nez Perce riders had brought them superb intelligence, but the Mounted Police had been following the campaign for months, and James Walsh and several officers had recently arrived. When word came that the Nez Perces were encircled three days' ride to the southwest, most of the refugees insisted on sending help. However, Walsh stood before the council and

---

[17] U.S. Commissioner of Indian Affairs, *Annual Report, 1877*, "Report of the Commission . . . ," 721. See also, N.A.C., File 2001, pt. 3a, "Macleod to Mills," 27 October 1877. See also U.S. Secretary of War, *Annual Report, 1877*, "Report of the General of the Army," "Howard to Sheridan," 19 October 1877, 76.

[18] U.S. Commissioner of Indian Affairs, *Annual Report, 1877*, "Report of the Commission . . . ," 722.

[19] U.S. Secretary of War, *Annual Report, 1877*, "Howard to Sheridan."

Brig. Gen. Alfred Terry, U.S. Army, commander of the Department of the Dakota and head of the Commission to the Sioux in the Northwest Territories in 1877. Photograph courtesy of the U.S. Library of Congress.

Col. Nelson A. Miles, commander of the Fifth Infantry and, later, the District of the Yellowstone. Photograph was taken in 1876 when Miles was thirty-seven years old. Photograph courtesy of the Montana Historical Society, Helena, Montana (L. A. Huffman photo).

A diet of horses and mules: photograph taken during George Crook's starvation march through the western Dakotas in 1876. Except for the engagement near Slim Buttes, the Sioux always seemed to be a step ahead of the soldiers. Photograph courtesy of the U.S. National Archives.

The commissioned officers of the Fifth Infantry at the start of the Wolf Mountain campaign in the winter of 1877. Miles is at center, wearing the "bearcoat," a greatcoat with a bear-fur collar. To his left is Lt. Frank Baldwin. To Miles's far left is Lt. George Baird. A note on the photograph says, "It was 20 below zero. . . ." Photograph courtesy of the U.S. National Archives.

Several Napoleon guns comprising the artillery section of the Fifth Infantry. Photograph was taken on the same day that Miles's troops moved up the Tongue River to engage the Sioux at Wolf Mountain. Photograph courtesy of the U.S. National Archives.

The Tongue River cantonment in late 1876. Located on the confluence of the Tongue and Yellowstone rivers, it was the headquarters for the Fifth Infantry. Photograph courtesy of the U.S. National Archives.

The Tongue River cantonment, later named Fort Keogh, in late 1877. Photograph courtesy of the U.S. National Archives.

The steamer "Rosebud" unloading supplies for the troops in the Yellowstone River valley in 1878. Photograph courtesy of the U.S. National Archives.

Elements of the Fifth Infantry operating to the north of the Yellowstone River in 1878. Photograph courtesy of the U.S. National Archives.

Fort Benton, Montana, in 1878. The steamer docked on the bank of the Missouri River is identified as the "Benton II." Photograph courtesy of the Montana Historical Society, Helena, Montana.

Fort Walsh in 1878. The post sat in a narrow valley between two spurs of the Cypress Hills, a well-watered island of pines and high ground on the Northern Plains. Photograph courtesy of the National Archives of Canada (negative no. C6547).

Left. James M. Walsh, superintendent, North-West Mountain Police. Although a note indicates that this photograph was taken near Wood Mountain, it may be a studio shot. Photograph courtesy of Saskatchewan Archives Board (photo no. R-859).

The Sioux headman Shanka Hoska and scout George Wells. The whitewashed log wall at their backs is similar to the construction at Fort Walsh. Photograph courtesy of the National Archives of Canada (negative no. PA38537).

A Mounted Police officer visiting with a Sioux Indian in 1878. The terrain in the background is similar to that of the Wood Mountain area. Photograph courtesy of the National Archives of Canada (negative no. C9570).

A Mounted Police officer visiting a Sioux encampment in the late 1870s. A note suggests that this photograph was taken in the Cypress Hills near Fort Walsh. Photograph courtesy of the Glenbow Archives, Calgary, Alberta, Canada.

Noncommissioned officers of the North-West Mounted Police at Fort Walsh, 1878. Photograph courtesy of the Glenbow Archives, Calgary, Alberta, Canada.

Canadian Minister of the Interior David Mills, photographed in January 1877. Photograph courtesy of the National Archives of Canada (negative no. PA33617).

U.S. Secretary of State William Evarts. Photograph courtesy of the U.S. Library of Congress.

Assistant Commissioner A. G. Irvine of the North-West Mounted Police. Photograph courtesy of the National Archives of Canada (negative no. PA42139).

Commissioner James F. Macleod of the North-West Mounted Police. Photograph courtesy of the National Archives of Canada (negative no. C17494).

OPPOSITE:

Left. U.S. Secretary of the Interior Carl Schurz. Photograph courtesy of the U.S. Library of Congress.

Right. Edward Thornton, British minister to the United States. Photograph courtesy of the U.S. Library of Congress.

Sitting Bull and Sioux leaders visiting Fort Walsh in 1878. Photograph was taken in Barracks Square inside the fort. The man seated to the right of the pole at center, wearing a light blanket with a dark stripe, may be Sitting Bull. To the right of "Sitting Bull" stands a mustachioed police officer in a braided coat and pith helmet. This person may be James Walsh. Photograph courtesy of National Archives of Canada (negative no. C19024).

The Mounted Police post at Wood Mountain in 1888. Photograph courtesy of Glenbow Archives, Calgary, Alberta, Canada.

Commissioned officers of the North-West Mounted Police at Fort Walsh in 1880. L. N. F. Crozier is seated at center. Photograph courtesy of National Archives of Canada (negative no. C19018C).

"F" Division of the North-West Mounted Police, 1881, James Walsh, Commander. Photograph was taken on the flats near Fort Walsh. Photograph courtesy of the National Archives of Canada (negative no. C19016B).

A formal portrait of James Walsh, probably taken after the Sioux had returned to the United States. Photograph courtesy of the National Archives of Canada (negative no. C17038).

Gall. Photograph was taken at Fort Buford, Dakota Territory, in May 1881, a short time after the Sioux headman had returned from Canada. Photograph courtesy of the U.S. National Archives.

Sitting Bull and members of his family under guard by the Twenty-Fifth Infantry at Fort Randall, Dakota Territory, in 1882. The white woman and children are unidentified; the officer on horseback is identified as "Captain Bentzoni" of Company "B," Twenty-Fifth Infantry. Photograph courtesy of the U.S. National Archives.

A formal portrait of Sitting Bull taken at Fort Randall in 1882, after the headman had returned from Canada. Photograph courtesy of the U.S. National Archives.

reminded the Sioux that if they crossed the border in force they would forfeit their privilege to live in peace in the Northwest Territories. The Mounted Police would prevent them from returning and their women and children would be forced over the border to join them. One of the officers present later wrote:

> The first day passed. No Indians left the camp. Gray dawn was appearing on the second day before the council adjourned. We slept until a few hours after sunrise. . . . At the end of the second day the Indians about concluded that it would be suicide for them . . . to render any help to the Nez Perce.[20]

The decision ended any chance of organized escape for the Nez Perces.[21] But the Nez Perces still hoped for assistance. A dispatch from Miles on October 3 reported:

> Joseph gave his solemn pledge yesterday that he would surrender, but did not, and they are evidently waiting for aid from other Indians. They say the Sioux are coming to their aid. I believe there is communication between their camp and Sitting Bull, and I have used every effort to prevent a junction. . . . I would respectfully suggest that information be sent to the British Authorities to prevent any portion of the Nez Perce tribe crossing the line, or disarm them should they take refuge on English soil.[22]

Joseph and the majority of the Nez Perces had already surrendered by the time Frederick Plunkett submitted Miles's request to the Canadian government. A few groups managed to elude the cordon of troops, and many of these Indians died trying to reach the border, victims of exposure or wounds, or roving parties of Assiniboines or Gros Ventres. Some were rounded up by patrols that Miles sent out after them. Most crossed into the Northwest Territories after much hardship, the largest group led by the Nez Perce headman White Bird.[23]

[20] Glenbow Archives, "Anonymous, letter to Cora [Walsh]," 34–35.

[21] Josephy, *Nez Perce Indians*, 608.

[22] N.A.C., RG 7, File 2001, pt. 3a, "Plunkett to W. B. Richards," 9 October 1877.

[23] Some accounts of the Bear Paws battle have suggested that Sitting Bull organized a large group of warriors go to their aid, but did not accompany them. This party met White Bird's group near the border and learned of Joseph's surrender. This version may be distorted. James Walsh was in Sitting Bull's camp at the time of White Bird's arrival and his account is corroborated by a letter to his daughter in 1890, from an anonymous Mounted Police officer who claimed to be present at Wood Mountain.

The arrival of these refugees to the camps of the Sioux came at an inopportune time. After concluding negotiations with the Canadian Blackfeet, James Macleod arrived at Fort Walsh to receive the American commission, only to find that the commissioners had been delayed in Fort Benton. Macleod decided to follow Superintendent Walsh to Wood Mountain because he was worried about the rumors that Sitting Bull might lead his warriors to the Bear Paws. But after riding east for a day, he met Walsh, who was returning with Sitting Bull and twenty other refugees.

Walsh had talked at great length to convince the Sioux to come to Fort Walsh. The Indians believed that American soldiers were nearby, and suspected that the meeting with the commissioners was an elaborate ruse to trap their leaders. The news of the Nez Perces' predicament across the border heightened their suspicions. Walsh was able to convince them that the Mounted Police would guarantee their safety and they finally agreed to go. Even so, "they were continually stopping to smoke and reconsider their decision."[24]

On the morning of their departure for Fort Walsh, some delay occurred when the headmen insisted upon waiting for their scouts to return to camp. They were still reluctant to go, but Walsh thought he had things under control. Suddenly two riders arrived, with reports of a large group of white men approaching from the south. The refugees feared the worst: "The horses were driven in, and the warriors mounted their horses and started off in the direction of the approaching Party. The women commenced taking down the lodges and packing up." Walsh tried to tell them that no white man would dare do them harm in the Northwest Territories, but the Indians refused to believe him. He offered to ride out and meet the incoming party, which "appeared to please them very much." With two hundred Indians riding behind, Walsh rode south for two miles, until he met a third Sioux scout, who told him that a group of Nez Perces was coming. "I waited their arrival," Walsh wrote, "and found the party to consist of fifty men, forty women, and a large number of children, besides about three hundred horses. Many of them were wounded men and children, some badly, some through the body, arms and legs."

Walsh took the Nez Perces back to the Sioux camp, where they were distributed among the lodges of the refugees for care. The sight of the ragged, bleeding band enraged the Sioux. The headmen confronted Walsh and demanded:

[24] N.A.C., RG 7, file 2001, pt. 3a, "Macleod to Mills," 27 October 1877.

Why do you come and seek us to go and talk with men who are kill-ing our race? You see these men, women and children wounded and bleeding? We cannot talk to men who have blood on their hands. They have stained the grass of the [Queen] with it.

Again, Walsh tried to convince them to meet with the American com-missioners:

I came here and asked you to come to one of the white mother's fort to meet a Commission sent to talk with you about returning to your own country. You need not accept their offers unless you like. You will not be forced to do so, but if you refuse to come to the fort of the white mother you will be the first to ever have done so![25]

For a few minutes the Sioux remained silent. Then, after a quiet con-versation among themselves, they agreed to go. It is likely that they intended only to please Walsh. The appearance and condition of the Bear Paws survivors probably eradicated any chance that the Sioux would accept the American terms of surrender.

When Macleod met them on the trail to the fort, the Sioux were once again having doubts. Macleod assured them that when they had "passed the line there as a wall raised up behind them that their enemies dared not cross." This seemed to satisfy them, and there was no further trouble until the party reached Fort Walsh. When the Sioux were invited to camp inside, Sitting Bull refused. Macleod prom-ised him that the Americans had not yet arrived, and to prove it, the commissioner ordered the entire contingent of Mounted Police out-side. Only when Sitting Bull had shaken the hand of every policeman did he consent to enter.

That evening, a courier rode in with a note from Terry announc-ing that the commission should arrive at the border on October 14. Macleod left the next morning with a Mounted Police escort. As soon as he was gone, the Indians' misgivings surfaced once again. The meeting would be useless, Sitting Bull stated; the Americans could not be trusted. Walsh managed to convince the Sioux to stay, but it was apparent to him that the meeting with the commission would amount to little more than an empty gesture.[26]

Dispatches from Miles had arrived in Fort Benton on October 8, reporting on Joseph's surrender, and telling Terry that the commission's escort would be available in a few days. But Terry was impatient. Rather than wait, he decided to meet the soldiers on the

[25] Much of this account can be found in "Sitting Bull Commission: Details of the Interview," quoting a letter from James Walsh to the Canadian Secretary of State, 12 October 1877, *Chicago Times*, 17 October 1877.

[26] N.A.C., RG 7, file 2001, pt. 3a, "Macleod to Mills," 27 October 1877.

way to the border. The commission left Fort Benton on October 10, and intercepted the escort two days later. On October 15 they reached the border where the contingent of Mounted Police was waiting. The army escort turned back, and Macleod and the commissioners rode into Fort Walsh the next day.[27]

At 10 o'clock the following morning, the commissioners met with the interpreters: their own, another in the employ of the Mounted Police, and a third brought along by the Sioux. The interpreters were familiarized with the commission's instructions, and the address that Terry would deliver to the Indians. The meeting began at three o'clock that afternoon in Walsh's quarters, a cramped apartment with a large front room. In attendance were the two American commissioners, Terry's secretary, Capt. H. C. Corbin, and Jay Stone, who acted as a recorder. Macleod, Walsh, and several officers of the Mounted Police were also present. The headmen present were Bear's Head, Spotted Eagle, Flying Bird, Whirlwind Bear, The-Medicine-Turns-Around, Iron Dog, The-Man-that-Scatters-the-Bear, Little Knife, The Crow, Yellow Dog, and Sitting Bull. The commissioners began by telling the Indians that Baptiste Shane, an American interpreter, would translate and the other two interpreters could listen for purposes of verification.

There was little ceremony. Terry simply stood and read aloud the propositions offered by the U.S. government:

> The President has instructed us to say to you that he desires to make a lasting peace with you and your people; he desires that all hostilities shall cease, and that all the people of the United States shall live together in harmony. He wishes this not for the sake of the whites alone, but for your sake as well; and he has instructed us to say that if you will return to your country, and hereafter refrain from acts of hostility against its government and people, a full pardon will be given to you for all acts committed in the past; that no matter what those acts have been, no attempt will be made to punish you or any man among you; that what is past shall be forgotten, and that you shall be received in the friendly spirit in which the other Indians who have been engaged in hostilities against the United States and have surrendered to its military forces have been received.

Of the Sioux who had already surrendered, "every man, every woman, and every child has been received as a friend," Terry claimed. The general then stipulated that the refugees must give up their arms and

[27] U.S. Commissioner of Indian Affairs, *Annual Report, 1877*, "Report of the Commission, . . ." 722–30. The following account in the text is taken from this document.

horses if they wished to return to the United States. It was time, Terry announced, for the Sioux to learn how to support themselves by raising cattle. The government had already brought several herds onto the reservations. The refugees would be provided with rations, clothing, and shelter until they could produce enough for their own needs.

The Sioux could not hold out much longer in the Northwest Territories, Terry claimed, for game was rapidly disappearing and soon they would starve. If they tried to return across the border on their own, they would be treated as enemies of the United States. "We ask you to take these propositions into consideration," Terry concluded, "to take time, consult together, and weigh them carefully. When you have done so, we shall be glad to meet you and receive your answer."

The gathered headmen needed no time to consider. Sitting Bull stood up and said:

> For sixty-four years you have kept me and my people and treated us bad. What have we done that you should want us to stop? We have done nothing. It is all the people on your side that have started us to do all these depredations. . . . You see me? Here I am! If you think I am a fool you are a bigger fool than I am. This house is a medicine house. You come here to tell us lies, but we don't want to hear them. . . . Don't you say two more words. Go back home where you came from. This country is mine, and I intend to stay here, and to raise this country full of grown people.

Sitting Bull claimed that he had been "raised" with the British in Canada, and to emphasize the point, shook hands with several police officers. Then, taking hands with another Indian in the room, he introduced him as a Santee Sioux who would "tell you something" about how the Santees felt.

The man identified himself as "The-One-that-Runs-the-Ree," and told a similar story:

> This country is ours. We did not give it to you. You stole it away from us. You have come over here to our country to tell us lies, and I don't propose to talk much, and that is all I have to say.

Nine, a Yankton, rose and repeated similar sentiments:

> This country over here is mine. The bullets I have over here I intend to kill something to eat with; not to kill anybody with them. That is what these people [the Mounted Police] told me; to kill nothing but what I wanted to eat with the ammunition they gave me. I will do so.

The wife of "The Man-that-Scatters-the-Bear" spoke next. She told the commissioners that she had wanted to remain in the United

States to "raise my children and have a little peace." That was impossible, so now she was determined to stay in Canada. Flying Bird concluded: "We have a little sense and we ought to love one another. Sitting Bull here says that whenever you found us out, wherever his country was, why, you wanted to have it." He would remain in the Northwest Territories, he stated, and shook the hands of several Mounted Police officers.

The Sioux rose as if to leave. Terry asked if this meant that the headman had refused the terms of surrender. Sitting Bull replied:

> I could tell you more, but that is all I have to tell you. If we told you more—why, you would not pay attention to it. That is all I have to say. This part of the country does not belong to your people. You belong on the other side; this side belongs to us.

The Crow claimed that his people had crossed the boundary into the United States because they thought "your people would take good care of [us]." On the other hand, the Canadians "over here gave me good care." The Canadians "don't hide anything," he said, and they "respected" Indians.

> I came over to this country, and my great mother knows all about it. She knows I came back over here, and she don't wish anything of me. We think, and all the women in the camp thinks, we are going to have a country full of people.

The Indians asked the commissioners if they had anything more to say. Terry and Lawrence did not, and the conference ended. Duty had been discharged.

The commissioners left the next morning. They reached Fort Benton on October 23, and hired mackinaw boats for the trip down the Missouri River to Fort Buford in Dakota Territory. There they boarded a Northern Pacific train for Saint Paul.[28] They arrived to find a letter from James Macleod waiting for them at departmental headquarters. The police officer had met with the Sioux headmen to make sure that the Indians understood the implications of their decision:

> The answer you have given to the United States Commissioners today prevents your ever going back to the United States with arms and ammunition in your possession. It is our duty to prevent you from doing this. I wish to tell you that if any of you or your young men cross the line with arms in your hand that then we become your enemies as well as the Americans.

[28] This ends the account of the "Report of the Commission. . . . "

> You must remember that you will live by the buffalo on this side of the line, and that the buffalo will not last forever. In a very few years they will all be killed. I hope you have thought well on the decision you have given today, not only for yourselves, but for your women and children.

Macleod's warning was clear: the Sioux would receive no more recognition from the Canadian government than that of refugees, and no support would be given to them. But Sitting Bull maintained that the Americans were untrustworthy. He was willing to live under "the Queen's law," he told Macleod, and revealed that the Sioux had agreed to meet with the commissioners only out of respect for the Mounted Police. Several other headmen agreed.

The refugees would be of no further concern to American authorities, Macleod wrote: "I do not think there need be the least anxiety about any of these Indians crossing the line, at any rate for some time to come."[29] Terry and Lawrence agreed, with some reservations. In their final report, the commissioners stated that they were "convinced that Sitting Bull and the Indians with him will not seek to return to this country at present." Macleod's warning, along with the memories of Miles's campaign against them during the winter of 1876–77, would discourage the Indians from crossing the border. It was likely, the commissioners believed, that the fate of the Sioux would be similar to that of the 1862 Minnesota War refugees, who could now be barely distinguished from other native peoples of the Canadian plains.

Until the Sioux grew "accustomed and attached" to their new home, the commissioners warned, they would remain "a standing menace to the peace." Yanktons, Assiniboines, and other groups lived on reservations close to the border, Terry and Lawrence pointed out, and could be susceptible to Sitting Bull's influence. His camp would continue to be an asylum for "the lawless and ill-disposed, [and] those who commit offenses against the property and persons of the whites." These "evils," the commissioners advised,

> may be in some degree avoided by a compliance on the part of the authorities of the Dominion of Canada with the rule of international law which requires that armed military or insurgent bodies which are driven by force across the frontier of a neutral state shall be "interned," shall be removed so far into the interior of the neutral

[29] N.A.C., RG 7, file 2001, pt. 3a, "Macleod to the Department of the Interior (Canada)," 17 October 1877.

state that they can no longer threaten . . . the state from which they came.[30]

That rule of international law was recognized in 1877, although codification would not be completed until forty-five years later, under the League of Nations. By the late nineteenth century certain concepts concerning the responsibilities of neutral states toward nations in conflict were generally accepted. A precedent in Anglo-American relations had been established several years before, when various disputes between the United States and Great Britain arising out of the Civil War had been settled by treaty and arbitration.[31] While there may have been parallels between cases involving arming Confederate ships for war and arming Sioux refugees for hunting, the commissioners' comparisons were probably irrelevant. The vague status of the Indians confused the issue. They were a native aborigine group under arms. In 1877, no special compacts or precedents covered their situation.

By granting the Sioux asylum, however, Canadian authorities gave themselves additional responsibilities. Chief among these was the obligation of the Dominion to prevent its territory from being used as a base for hostile operations. If necessary, surveillance, internment, and even incarceration could be used to inhibit this activity.[32] This was the position staked out by Carl Schurz, and it did not differ substantially from the recommendations of the commissioners. The commission had been orchestrated for the good will of Great Britain and Canada. For the United States government, it could not fail. It appeased the British and Canadians, and served notice to the Sioux. If the Indians chose to surrender, the U.S. Army could be employed to incarcerate them. If they refused to surrender, Canada might have no choice but to intern them away from the border. If the Dominion refused to take action, then the weight of international precedent would be against them.

The Canadian approach did not follow the American prescription, however. Ottawa sought no long-term solutions, only temporary accommodations. The Sioux would not receive support, nor

[30] U.S. Commissioner of Indian Affairs, *Annual Report, 1877*, "Report of the Commission . . . ," 722.

[31] Department of State, *The Case of the United States to be Laid Before the Tribunal of Arbitration to be Convened at Geneva* (Washington, D.C.: Government Printing Office, 1872), part 3, p. 47.

[32] L. L. Oppenheim, *International Law: A Treatise*, vol. 2, "Disputes, War and Neutrality," ed. H. Lauterpacht (London: Longmans, Green and Co., 1955), 704. See also vol. 1, "Peace," 678.

would an attempt be made to disarm and relocate them. Given the circumstances, it was probably impossible to do so. As Frederick Plunkett pointed out to the Earl of Derby in October: "If Canada is to be held responsible for [the refugees'] good behaviour, she must increase enormously her military force in that country."[33] Canadian officials hoped that this would not be necessary, that further negotiations might lead to an agreement, or that Great Britain might absorb some of the cost of policing the Indians. But Macleod and others realized that time was short. When the buffalo and other game resources disappeared, the Sioux could hardly be expected to submit to starvation peacefully.

Sympathy for the Canadian position grew in British governmental circles. Plunkett had written to Derby: "It does not seem to me just that [Canada] should be put to such an enormous expense, because the United States does not keep the treaties which she has made with her Indian tribes." His remarks had made an impression. In a note to the Colonial Office in London, the undersecretary for the Foreign Office discussed taking a stand upon the issue, despite the need to maintain good Anglo-American relations:

> Mr. Plunkett's remarks to the effect that there appears to be a desire on the part of the American public to throw upon the Canadian Government the necessity of disarming the Indians who may be driven over the frontier, appear to Lord Carnarvon to demand attention. If, as there seems reason to apprehend, it should be contemplated or advocated by any influential persons in the States to force the Indians out of their own country across the Canadian frontier, in order that Canada should then be held responsible for the good behaviour of these Indians, it may deserve consideration whether an opportunity should not be taken of intimating to the United States Government that Canada cannot be expected to undertake any such responsibility[34]

In a short span of time, large groups from two tribes native to the United States had been forced over the border into the Northwest Territories. The Hayes administration had done nothing to dissuade the governments of Canada and Great Britain that this might not become American policy in the future.

As for the refugees, their intentions were clear. They would remain in Canada so long as the means for survival existed. The meeting with the American commissioners at Fort Walsh had been

[33] N.A.C., RG 7, file 2001, pt. 3d, "Plunkett to Dufferin," 9 October 1877.

[34] Ibid., "R. G. W. Herbert, Undersecretary of the Foreign Office, to the Colonial Office," 6 November 1877.

incredibly ill-timed. The arrival of wounded Nez Perce survivors at Wood Mountain had not made a good impression on the Sioux, while the stern address read by Terry as he stood in military uniform did not allay their fear and mistrust. By the time the commission convened, the refugees had heard of the death of Crazy Horse, who had surrendered and returned to reservations in the spring of 1877. By summer, the rumors spread that he planned to lead his people into the Powder River country again, or perhaps to Canada. He had been arrested on September 5, and when he resisted he was bayoneted to death. The consequences of his surrender could not have been lost on the Sioux at Wood Mountain.[35]

[35] Utley, *Frontier Regulars*, 282.

CHAPTER 5

"...These Reports Are
Wholly Unfounded..."

*RUMORS OF INVASION AND WAR,
WINTER AND SPRING 1878*

Reactions to the commission's failure varied. The *New York Herald* expressed satisfaction: "We wish the Great Mother joy with her new subjects." The *New York Times* agreed: "Their refusal to accept the terms presented by the Commission relieves this Government of all responsibility for them, and leaves them [in the] charge of the Dominion authorities." But the *Chicago Times* editorialized: "The Sioux would not entertain the propositions of the Commissioners at all, simply because, having had abundant experience of the bad faith of the U.S. government officials, they feared treachery." Sitting Bull expected and got "lies," the *Times* reported. The *New York Tribune* opined that the Indians' attitudes were justified by their shabby treatment in the United States:

> When Indian chiefs successively shook hands with the British officers present at the conference . . . and expressed their intention of living in peace under the protection of the Great Mother, it was a sad

commentary on our own Indian policy that we could not but acknowl-
edge that there they might find peace and safety, and there only.[1]

The former abolitionist Wendell Phillips took a similar position
when he jumped into the controversy that summer. In a letter to the
governor-general of Canada, Phillips implored Dufferin to remember
British traditions:

> It has been England's pride for centuries that her borders were ever
> the shelter for the victims of political misrule; that while she surren-
> dered ordinary criminals, she never gave up the defeated parties of a
> civil war or any like struggle.

Phillips argued that the Sioux refugees were not ordinary criminals
since the United States government had negotiated treaties with their
tribe, and held individual members subject to the authority of an
"irregular tribal government." When the United States made war on
the Sioux, the refugees chose to exile themselves rather than surrender. To Phillips, the political connotations of their exile were clear.
The former abolitionist's entreaty to Dufferin took on a tone of florid
sermonizing:

> Every reason which made England refuse to give up the fugitive
> slave exists in the Indian's case, and there are some considerations
> which make his claim to protection even stronger than the negro's
> was. I beseech you, sir, let not the first time that England's magna-
> nimity in this way fails be in the case of this friendless and hunted
> race, crushed out and trodden down alike by the greed and neglect
> of a powerful and grasping people.[2]

Ironically, Phillips envisioned a solution very much like the one the
Hayes administration hoped for: intern the Sioux on a reserve in
Canada permanently. But Dufferin's view remained unchanged: the
Indians would be tolerated and extended temporary protection, more
because of delicate relations with the United States than for human-
itarian reasons.

As a news item, the situation at Wood Mountain might have
faded into relative obscurity after the commission returned, had it
not been for consistent rumors about raids into Montana and Sitting
Bull's repeated attempts to build an alliance of disaffected Northern

[1] Untitled editorial, *New York Herald*, 23 October 1877; "The Sitting Bull
Conference," *New York Times*, 27 October 1877; "The Failure of the Sitting Bull
Commission," *Chicago Times*, 27 October 1877; "Sitting Bull Commission: Details
of the Interview," *Chicago Times*, 17 October 1877; "A Lesson from the Savages,"
New York Tribune, 24 October 1877.

[2] "Sitting Bull," *Manitoba Daily Free Press*, 23 August 1877.

Plains tribes. The Nez Perces' attempt to join the Sioux and reports that the Canadian Blackfeet were dissatisfied with their treaty with Canada fueled speculations. Army officers in the District of the Yellowstone gave the speculations credibility by taking them seriously.

Especially aggravating were the inflated editorials and stories printed by the *Benton Record,* which Col. Nelson Miles often quoted to his superiors. The *Record* wanted a military post built on the Milk River to shut off this "convenient avenue of escape to the British Possessions" by "renegade" tribes. Logistically, the point of supply for such a facility would be Fort Benton, and the town would profit from it. As a result, the editors of the *Record* often manufactured trouble: Sitting Bull and thousands of warriors were reported to be camped on the Milk or Marias rivers, raiding outlying ranches, hijacking wagons and stages, and threatening to overrun the town of Fort Benton itself.[3]

Miles used these reports for his own purposes, as did Montana Congressional representative Martin MacGinnis. In testimony before the House Army Appropriations Committee MacGinnis ridiculed the belief that

> we will have no more trouble with Sitting Bull, as he is beyond the Canadian border. But what is he doing there? He is endeavouring to organize the Northwest Tribes, and if he succeeds he can march a force of ten thousand men, equal to any soldiers you can put in the field, and sweep every settlement before him; he can clean the country out from the line to the railroad before you can organize to stop him. Do you think that because he is on that side of the line his respect for Queen Victoria or a squadron of Canadian Policemen will stop him?[4]

MacGinnis's solution was predictable: army garrisons in Montana should be reinforced, and new posts should be built. It was an old game—create an Indian scare for the sake of economic prosperity that army protection might bring. One by-product was a high level of tension in Montana; another was continued attention to the events along the border by the national press.

None of this impressed the Canadians. The *Manitoba Daily Free Press* regularly poked fun at the residents of Fort Benton for believ-

[3] "Reasons for Establishing a Fort on the Milk River," *Benton Record,* 26 October 1877, "Snake Creek Battle," 12 October 1877, "Sioux," 23 November 1877, "Our Unprotected Border," 17 December 1877, "Our Threatened Border," 21 December 1877.

[4] "Congressional," *Benton Record,* 30 November 1877.

ing everything they heard. The *Press* gleefully related the details of one incident. According to the newspaper, James Walsh made a practice of paying Indians for information, but sometimes the intelligence he bought was less than accurate. An Assiniboine named "Turtle-Who-Eats-Dirt" rode into Fort Walsh and claimed that Sitting Bull had visited the different tribes in the area in an effort to unite them for a general war against the whites. Turtle said that Sitting Bull had sent the tribal headmen "big pieces of paper" on which was printed an appeal for an alliance and a date for the war to begin. When Walsh asked him to produce a "big piece of paper," Turtle gave him two posters. The first read:

LISEZ! LISEZ! LISEZ! Le plus Énergique des Désinfectants! Un novelle préparation recommende par les premieres chimistes . . . ,

which was simply an advertisement for a Winnipeg druggist selling insect poison. The other poster showed a medallion from the latest Paris industrial exposition and advertised the merits of *"la véritable machine à coudre Américaine par Elias Howe."* The *Press* claimed that the citizens of Fort Benton had received a distorted version of this affair and panicked.[5]

The *Press* was not impressed by arguments that the Sioux refugees should become permanent residents of the Canadian plains. Responding to Wendell Phillips's arguments that the Indians might be considered as defeated parties of a civil war, or individuals of a nation hostile to the United States, or persecuted fugitives similar to escaped slaves, the newspaper commented that "Mr. Phillips' appeal [can] only be characterised as an outburst of feeling from an ultraphilanthropist." The Sioux were not citizens of the United States, the *Press* pointed out, and could not be parties to a civil war. They were "wards" of the United States government, which was liable for them, "as they would be in the case of adolescents not arrived at their majority or of foreigners, Irish, German or others, domiciled in the United States who might use their territories as a basis of operations against other countries."[6]

The *Press* described the Sioux as armed warriors who had been victorious against the American army, and who had chosen exile voluntarily. They were not persecuted fugitives. "The United States," the *Press* editorialized, "has assumed the responsibility while assuming [Sioux] land; and for no unabetted act of [these Indians] can any

[5] "How a Sensational Report Originated," *Manitoba Daily Free Press*, 10 October 1877.

[6] "Sioux Repatriation," ibid., 6 September 1877.

other than the United States authorities be held responsible." Canada was the damaged party in this dispute, the newspaper claimed. Referring to the furor in the United States over Kickapoo and Comanche raids into Texas from Mexican territory, the *Press* concluded:

> [Mexico] has all along expressed regret at the perpetration of border raids and at its inability to control its Indians, which is no offense more serious than that of the Americans in failing to hold in check their Sioux, their Nez Perces, their Fenians.[7]

None of this halted the proliferating rumors, and several kept the border area in turmoil as diplomatic notes passed back and forth between the Department of State and the British Legation in Washington. In November 1877 the *New York World* published a report that the Canadian government had acquiesced to Carl Schurz's request that the Sioux be moved away from the border and given a reservation. Other newspapers quickly picked it up. The *New York Times* suggested that if the Canadians balked at the expense involved, the United States should be willing to pay a portion. In Montana, the *Helena Herald* called for a reserve as far north of the border as possible. The *New North-West* quoted James Walsh as saying that the Sioux would be resettled on the Souris River in the Dirt Hills. But when other reports described large Sioux hunting parties in northern Montana, this rumor died quickly.[8]

Another rumor involved Corp. Martin Ryan, an alleged survivor of the Little Bighorn who had supposedly been captured and forced to marry a Sioux woman. He was, according to the stories, currently being held in a camp at Wood Mountain where Baptiste Shane had spoken with him. Shane told General Terry, and a check of the records revealed that a Corp. Martin Ryan of Company "C" of the Seventh Cavalry was listed as killed in action. Terry wrote a letter to army headquarters in Saint Louis, observing that since Ryan was an American soldier, Canadian officials had a responsibility to try and "liberate" him. The adjutant general passed the letter on to the Department of State, and William Evarts sent a note to the minister of the British Legation, Edward Thornton. Eventually, a request for information on Corporal Ryan reached the Mounted Police, and A. G. Irvine set out from Fort Walsh to investigate.

[7] "An Invasion of Mexico," ibid., 9 October 1877.
[8] "Relocation," *New York World*, 11 November 1877; "Sitting Bull," *New York Times*, 14 November 1877; Untitled, *Helena Herald*, 20 October 1877; "Sitting Bull," *New North-West*, 2 November 1877.

Irvine found no captive soldier at Wood Mountain. Sitting Bull denied that prisoners had been taken at the Little Bighorn, and Spotted Eagle, reportedly the father of the woman Ryan was forced to marry, had only a fifteen-year-old son. The Métis traders who sold guns and ammunition to the Sioux denied any knowledge of a white man living with the Indians. When Irvine returned to Fort Walsh in February 1878, he declared the rumor to be false.[9]

Far more serious were the rumors that the Sioux were preparing to move back across the border in force. Some of these stories probably had their origins in the editorial offices of the *Benton Record*. The *New York Times* and other eastern newspapers reported that Sitting Bull had formed an alliance with the Blackfeet and the Crees, and was negotiating with the Assiniboines, Yanktons, and other tribes in Montana. The alliance would attack Fort Walsh and Fort Macleod first, and once they had finished with the Mounted Police they would march south and engage the U.S. Army. It appeared that the much-heralded general Indian war was about to break out, at least in the collective imagination of the American press.[10]

Early in January 1878, Colonel Miles wrote another in a series of long personal letters to General Sherman, who happened to be his wife's uncle. He reported that Sitting Bull had recently crossed the border with two thousand warriors, intent upon destroying Fort Benton and the reservation agencies at Fort Belknap and Fort Peck. Miles noted sarcastically that it would be "somewhat discouraging" to take out a few hundred troops to oppose this invasion, and pointed out that there were nearly two thousand soldiers on his eastern flank doing nothing but camping on the reservations and guarding train stations. "If I have not earned a [proper] command, I never shall," concluded the colonel; "now suppose you give me one chance at this business alone."[11]

Sherman archly responded, "I am always glad to hear from you Miles, and of you, but of late you have introduced into your letters too much important official matters. . . . It is not right that we should correspond on subjects direct." After stating that he would not make Miles "a Brigadier General . . . nor advise a new department for your special command," Sherman warned the colonel not to venture near the border:

[9] N.A.C., RG 7, file 2001, pt. 3d, "Thornton to Evarts," 1 December 1877.

[10] "Sitting Bull Prepares for War," *New York Times*, 21 March 1878, "Sitting Bull's Sioux Plotting," 9 February 1878.

[11] Library of Congress, "William T. Sherman papers," vol. 47, "Miles to Sherman," 8 January 1878.

I doubt if you should carry winter operations north of the Missouri
River, and most undoubtedly were you, without the positive orders
of the Government here in Washington, to cross the British Line on
the theory that the Canadian authorities are not acting in good faith,
you would endanger the high reputation you now possess.[12]

Apparently, the warning was necessary. On several occasions
Miles had publicly stated that the U.S. Army should have the right to
follow raiding groups of Indians across international boundaries, if in
hot pursuit. As a precedent, he cited long-standing practices among
army units stationed along the Rio Grande. In one sense, the colonel
had already flouted Canadian sovereignty by operating an intelligence network that extended into the Northwest Territories. The network, which probably consisted of scouts and paid Indian informers,
even helped Miles's staff to prepare a summary of the tactical condition of the Mounted Police at Fort Macleod and Fort Walsh.[13]

Sherman knew that violating the territorial integrity of a weak
nation like Mexico while pursuing bandits and fugitives was very different from infringing upon the lands of a great power to punish refugees. On the southern border the United States might act with relative impunity, but on the northern border, as several Canadian
newspapers had already pointed out, "a nation that invades a
neighbouring country with which it is at peace; even in the pursuit of
thieves and ruffians, must be fully prepared to stand the natural consequences of an act of open hostility."[14] Miles, Sherman realized, did
not respect the intricacies of international hierarchy. The colonel
deserved careful supervision.

Nevertheless, the prospect of two thousand warriors pillaging
Montana concerned the general, and he sent notes to George McCrary and William Evarts suggesting that the Canadian government be
asked to find out where the Sioux were. But Evarts had already acted.
In December 1877, McCrary received a message from the District of
the Yellowstone that two Cheyennes at Fort Keogh claimed to have
met a Sioux refugee while camping near Fort Berthold. The refugee
told them that "171 Indian tribes" were assembled north of the border, and "it was the intention of Sitting Bull to come south and fight
in the middle of the whites." At the same time, Miles's Cheyenne
scouts informed the colonel that large numbers of Sioux were leaving the Missouri River reservations; among them were two hundred
lodges led by Little Hawk, the uncle of Crazy Horse. Department of

[12] Ibid., vol. 90, "Sherman to Miles," 9 February 1878.
[13] N.A.R.A., RG 393, District of the Yellowstone, 1876–1881, Letters and Telegrams Received, 1876–1881, "Canada—North-West Mounted Police Force," n.d.
[14] "An Invasion of Mexico," *Manitoba Daily Free Press*, 9 October 1877.

the Dakota headquarters recommended that the agency staffs at Fort Belknap and Fort Peck be evacuated, along with the army garrison at Peck. Evarts handed these documents to Edward Thornton in early January, at about the same time that Miles wrote to Sherman.[15]

Canadian Secretary of State R. W. Scott telegraphed James Macleod asking if the reports were accurate. Macleod, who was visiting in Helena at the time, knew nothing about the events described. "My last reports from Fort Walsh give me no reason to believe that the state of affairs in that neighbourhood have changed," he wrote, "except that 60 lodges of Sioux had crossed the line and joined Sitting Bull's band." He told Scott that the source of these reports lay not at Wood Mountain, but in Fort Benton: "In fact there is no doubt that these reports are wholly unfounded—and that they are propagated by persons who are interested in the establishment of a military post in the neighbourhood of Fort Benton."[16]

Once again A. G. Irvine rode out to Wood Mountain to check upon the Sioux refugees. He found four hundred lodges scattered about the area. Sitting Bull and about thirty lodges of his people were quietly camped on a spot three miles from a small Mounted Police shack. At the other end of the hills, Spotted Eagle and approximately one hundred and fifty lodges were moving slowly west to join him. All forty-five of the Nez Perce lodges were in this group. There was no gathering of hostile tribes, and no evidence of an impending war.[17]

Evarts was not yet satisfied. Miles continued to forward reports of "hostile" bands of Indians roaming south of the border. In mid-February 1878, the colonel noted that four hundred and ten lodges had passed the garrison at Fort Peck on their way to join the refugees in Canada. Miles was quite sure about his information, although "whether the main hostile camp remains south or immediately north of the line . . . [it] endangers life and property in this region." After demanding that the Canadian government be given a deadline on April 10 to intern the Sioux away from the border, he asked permission to set up communications with the Mounted Police regarding movements of Indians in the area.[18]

Evarts met with Thornton and once more expressed concern that the refugees and their allies were preparing to "invade United States Territory." The secretary of state warned Thornton that the

[15] N.A.C., RG 7, file 2001, pt. 3a, "Thornton to Dufferin," 19 January 1878.
[16] Ibid., "Macleod to Scott," 22 January 1878.
[17] Ibid., "Irvine to Scott," 2 February 1878. See also ibid., pt. 3d, "Macleod to Scott," 29 January 1878.
[18] N.A.R.A., RG 393, District of the Yellowstone, Letters and Telegrams Sent, "Miles to Ruggle," 19 February 1878.

U.S. Army would repel the invasion with force, and in that case, continued sanctuary for the Sioux in Canada would be unacceptable to the United States government.[19] Thornton declared that the Mounted Police would do their best to prevent such an attack, but he reminded Evarts that the police were few in numbers and might be unsuccessful. Evarts suggested that the British Army be used to control the Indians, even if it meant calling in units from outside of North America.

Again, A. G. Irvine returned to Wood Mountain to assess the situation. This time he found four hundred and fifty Sioux lodges camped on the north side of the border. These were Crazy Horse's people, led by Little Hawk from the reservations in the Dakotas, the likely source of some of the rumors. They had been slowly moving northwest in search of Sitting Bull's encampment, and were relieved to learn that they had crossed the border at last. In a terse telegram to the Canadian Department of State, Irvine reported: "No danger of Canadian Indians making an alliance with Sioux against whites."[20]

After this episode, tensions in the border area gradually abated. The *New York Times* reluctantly admitted that stories of the refugees invading Montana were "exaggerated" and the Indians were "probably as peaceful as the Mounted Police report." But the newspaper warned that if an alliance was ever effected with the Canadian tribes, it would lead to "the most serious Indian war of the century."[21]

Only the *Benton Record* continued to lend credence to reports that the Sioux were operating south of the border. In the early spring of 1878, the newspaper took issue with the accounts of the Mounted Police. The Indians were "swarming" between the boundary and the Missouri River, the *Record* editorialized, yet nothing was being done because of "lying correspondents" of certain eastern newspapers, corruption in the federal government, and the cowardice of Col. John Gibbon, the commander of the District of Montana. "The [army] scouts confirmed our reports," the newspaper fulminated. "The public was given to understand that the people of Benton were liars. There is to be no campaign—not because there are no Indians, but because the Milk River country is full of them."[22]

Even Nelson Miles deserted the cause. When the colonel finally admitted that the refugees were living peacefully at Wood Mountain,

[19] N.A.C., RG 7, file 2001, pt. 3a, "Thornton to Dufferin," 4 February 1878.
[20] Ibid., pt. 3d, "Irvine to Scott," 2 March 1878.
[21] "The Indian Frontier Movements," *New York Times*, 29 April 1878.
[22] "A Pretty Story," *Benton Record*, 1 February 1878, "Indian News," 8 February 1878, "Sitting Bull," 8 February 1878, "The Situation," 1 March 1878, "Why There is No Campaign," 6 March 1878.

the *Record* fashioned new heights of journalistic convolution. Sitting Bull had lost prestige and influence over the refugees, the newspaper claimed, and did not accompany them into the Milk River area but remained at Wood Mountain in "mortal dread of American soldiers." A scout named Kaiser had misled Miles into believing that there were no hostile Sioux in northern Montana. This "licentious squaw lover" was seduced near Fort Clagett by the "dusky belles" of a Crow camp sympathetic to the refugees, "and after revelling in their charms until satiety permitted him to return to the Tongue River Post," he told Miles what the Crows had intended him to say. The publication of such a story was enough to make even Miles wary of the *Benton Record*, and his reports to department headquarters in Saint Paul became markedly more measured thereafter.[23]

The Sioux continued to live uneventfully in the Territories, unaware of the furor they were causing in the United States. A correspondent from the *New York Tribune* visited the camps that winter and found the Indians undisturbed and not very anxious about the situation. The Mounted Police had stepped up their campaign against the whiskey trade, and Sitting Bull, eager to cooperate, had enforced similar sanctions in his own camp. Because the Sioux were having trouble finding ammunition for their American-made Winchester and Spencer rifles, Métis traders sold them large numbers of British Enfields, at eight to twelve buffalo pelts apiece. The *Tribune* correspondent observed:

> Sitting Bull spends the day reading old newspapers, preparing herbs and roots for the old and sick among his people—for he is something of a medicine man—and talking to his headmen. The police visit him twice a week and sometimes oftener, and occasionally he returns the visit.[24]

The idyllic life at Wood Mountain was merely a bit of calm amidst the storm. The debate between governments over what to do about the Sioux had not yet affected them, but other factors had begun to. On the plains around them, and from within their own camps, their unity, security, and livelihood were already threatened. The hierarchy of leadership showed early signs of crumbling, and Sitting Bull appeared to be losing some control over the refugees. The headman's influence had never been absolute, and lesser chiefs and warriors often came and went as they pleased. But rival leaders began to compete with Sitting Bull at a time when two years of inaction had made him vulnerable. His plan for a confederacy of northwestern tribes

[23] "Sitting Bull," ibid., 8 February 1878, "Buell's Scouts," 8 February 1878.
[24] "Sitting Bull Snowbound," *New York Tribune*, 7 December 1877.

had failed. His position as leader of the confederacy had been usurped by the Cree headmen Big Bear and Poundmaker, who had led a revolt against the Dominion over new regulations governing buffalo hunting.[25]

In addition, Sitting Bull may have had a falling out with the Mounted Police, especially James Walsh. There were reports that Walsh publicly humiliated the headman in the midst of an argument over some food stores at Fort Walsh by bodily picking him up and throwing him through an office door.[26] Gradually, the police officers' attitudes had changed. Sympathy turned to toleration, and then to mild contempt, an evolution that reflected changes in attitudes and policies in Ottawa. Walsh labored to maintain good relations with the refugees, but his independence and his magnanimity toward them provoked distrust among his superiors, and his position would soon be compromised.

Finally, as predicted, hunger became a problem. By the summer of 1878, buffalo and other game were scarce in the territories, heralding hard times to come. Sitting Bull renewed his efforts to obtain supplies from the Dominion, but to no avail. That spring the Privy Council had reaffirmed the Canadian position: "[They are] refugees seeking temporary asylum" and not subject to the same rights and privileges given to Canadian tribes.[27] In June, Commissioner Macleod reported that buffalo and other sources of food were too scarce to allow for large encampments, so the Sioux had broken up and scattered across the country north of the Cypress Hills. Hunting and foraging difficulties and physical separation further eroded cohesion among the refugees. A gradual exodus began, as a few Indians trickled across the border and returned to the reservations.[28]

American authorities had not forgotten about the Sioux. In a note to Edward Thornton, Secretary of State William Evarts demanded that the British government pressure Canada to intern the Sioux in a place far away from the border. But Lord Dufferin and the Privy Council resolved that "it is not considered desirable that they should be located by the Government at present."[29] Cooperation at a lower level appeared easier. Colonel Miles had asked to be allowed to coor-

---

[25] R. G. MacBeth, *Policing the Plains* (Toronto: Musson Books, Ltd., 1931), 86.

[26] Paul F. Sharp, *Whoop-Up Country* (Minneapolis: University of Minnesota, 1955), 283. Sharp does not cite sources for this story.

[27] N.A.C., RG 7, file 2001, pt. 3a, "Copy of a Report of the Privy Council," 26 March 1878.

[28] Ibid., "Walsh to Scott," 23 June 1878.

[29] Ibid., "Evarts to Thornton," 18 March 1878; ibid., "Copy of a Report of the Privy Council," 26 March 1878.

dinate intelligence and surveillance operations with the Mounted Police.[30] The Privy Council had no objections, and forwarded instructions to Commissioner Macleod "to act in harmony with the United States forces in maintaining order on the frontier."[31]

The Department of the Dakota headquarters chose to regard this accommodation as permission to do some negotiating of its own. Miles's intelligence network picked up a rumor that the Nez Perce refugees wanted to join Joseph on the southern plains, and General Terry decided to send three of Joseph's people to Fort Keogh on the Tongue River with instructions that they be escorted to the border by one of Miles's officers. If the Mounted Police consented, the Indians and this officer would try to convince the Nez Perce to return to the United States. Macleod was informed of the plan before the party left Fort Keogh, and the commissioner sent A. G. Irvine to Wood Mountain to find the Nez Perce. Only twenty-five lodges remained; the rest had returned to the Lapwai reservation in Idaho that spring. Among those who remained was the headman White Bird, who believed that the Americans would kill him if he surrendered.[32]

On June 22, 1878, Lt. George W. Baird, two white scouts, and the three Indians from Joseph's camp in Kansas showed up at Fort Walsh. Macleod was happy to help, but he stipulated that only the three Nez Perce emissaries be sent to White Bird's camp, escorted by A. G. Irvine and a small contingent of police. Baird and his white scouts could not go, because the refugees disliked "American officers," and White Bird had said they were "not wanted back again."[33]

Irvine managed to convince White Bird and his people to return with him to Fort Walsh to meet with Baird and hear his offer. White Bird finally agreed to go out of courtesy to the Mounted Police, and because Irvine painted a positive picture of Joseph's exile at Leavenworth. The party returned to the fort on June 30, and the next morning Macleod, Irvine, and Baird met with White Bird and a few of his people in the front room of James Walsh's apartment. Macleod began by telling White Bird that the American officer had come to try to reach an agreement whereby the Nez Perce could return to the United States. He invited White Bird to express his

[30] N.A.R.A., RG 393, District of the Yellowstone, Letters and Telegrams Received, "Evarts to McCrary," 15 April 1878.

[31] N.A.C., RG 7, file 2001, pt. 3a, "Copy of a Report of the Privy Council," 26 March 1878.

[32] Ibid., "Macleod to Scott," 23 June 1878.

[33] N.A.R.A., RG 393, District of the Yellowstone, Letters and Telegrams Received, "Macleod to Baird," 22 June 1878.

opinion about the American offer to place the Nez Perces on their own reservation.[34]

"I want to know which way Joseph is going," White Bird said.

Baird replied, "I would rather hear all you have to say and then reply."

"Would you rather I should speak, or retire and hold a council with the others?" asked the headman.

"I would rather you do just as you please," answered Baird.

"I would rather hear you speak," said White Bird. "I want to hear what you are going to do with Joseph."

Baird claimed that Joseph's people were being treated well, and would soon be given a reservation of their own, "maybe at your old home." He assured the assembled Indians that everyone in the United States thought well of the Nez Perces, and wished them no harm. The Mounted Police could not supply the refugees with food, he pointed out, but if White Bird's people agreed to return with him, they would be restored to Joseph and given what they needed.

White Bird was glad to hear there was no more fighting and said that he was satisfied with Baird's offer, but he insisted that "I would like to see Joseph and like to see him back in his own country." Baird recommended that he return to the United States and see Joseph, pointing out that the three Nez Perce emissaries should convince the refugees that the U.S. government's intentions were benign.

White Bird then told Baird that he wanted to consult directly with Joseph about returning. Baird demurred, saying,

> You can talk among yourselves and make up your minds if you will come. I can tell Joseph what you said, but if you want to have Joseph know, you had better go yourselves. The Great Father did not send me here to hear what you had to say . . . but to take you down if you wanted to go.

He suggested that the Nez Perces use the rest of the day to discuss the matter among themselves.

On July 2, Macleod opened the second meeting by asking the refugees what they had decided. White Bird called upon the three Nez Perce emissaries to describe the surrender at the Bear Paws battlefield and tell what conditions were like among Joseph's people at Fort Leavenworth.

Yellow Bird, the first speaker, recalled that Miles had told Joseph that if he surrendered his people would be returned to their own

---

[34] Ibid., "Monday Morning," n.d., probably early July, 1878. The account of the meetings that follows in the text is taken from this document, a transcript of dialogue taken down in shorthand by a police officer and later transcribed.

country. Bald Head claimed to have been with Joseph when he surrendered to the Americans. After Joseph made his surrender speech, Colonel Miles had asked him, "Are you wide awake now? Do you see more now than before you fought?" Joseph had replied, "Yes, I see plainer now but we were both blind before. And now the country is like daylight, but before it was dark." Bald Head also declared that Miles had promised that the Nez Perces would be returned to their own country. The emissary said that Joseph was concerned about staying at Leavenworth "because it is not healthy. His people and children are dying. . . . Joseph surrendered to save his people and why should he go further south and let his people perish?" The third man confirmed what Yellow Bird and Bald Head said.

White Bird and his people were disturbed by this description of the dismal conditions at Leavenworth, and suspected that Miles' promises had been compromised. Baird took the offensive by testing the refugees' loyalties:

> If the White Bird and the Nez Perce who are with him will go over and join Joseph there is a very good prospect that they will go back [to Idaho], but if White Bird and his people stay here, there is not a good prospect that Joseph and his people will go back, and I will tell you why; because the Great Father may say: "White Bird and his people are living with my enemies the Sioux and as long as they live with my enemies I don't want Joseph and his people to go back to his old home."

But White Bird said that Joseph did not want to be sent into the southwestern plains:

> I hear that it is very bad country for them. For my part, I want Joseph to come back to our part of the country. I don't wish to stay with the Sioux. If Joseph comes back to our part of the country . . . I will join him. I don't like the Sioux and don't wish to stay with them. I don't care for the Sioux—I just camp there to pass the time. . . . I try to live in peace as the Mounted Police told me.

Macleod reminded White Bird that no formal peace agreement existed between the Nez Perce refugees and the U.S. government, and that the reason for Baird's presence was to negotiate such an agreement and take the Indians home. "I think it is a very kind and generous offer on behalf of the President," Macleod stated, "and if you do not accept it now, it may never occur again." He related that during the Terry commission's visit the year before he had told the Sioux that game animals would be their only source of support, and if the game disappeared, they would starve. "You are not deciding for today and yourselves," he said, "but for years to come and for your wives and children. . . . If you take my advice you will go there and be happy too." Macleod then adjourned the meeting for lunch.

By the afternoon, White Bird had made up his mind: "Since we talked this morning with you we went out and had a Council, and, for my part I do not want to go." He asked if a man could be sent down to see Joseph and report on conditions at Leavenworth—"I want to find out how my Indians are going to be treated." Baird flatly rejected the idea, calling it a waste of time. Then he turned to the other Indians, saying, "White Bird says he does not want to go back with me. If there are any who do wish to go back they can do so." Macleod emphasized this: "I would like to hear what the others have to say. Each one of you has to judge for himself. . . . A great many bad men throughout the country have been telling you lies, don't believe them; don't let those lies influence you."

Baird warned that anyone who slipped over the border intending to return to Lapwai would be "arrested as hostile Indians." He made it clear that his offer was the only way for the refugees to return to their people. But White Bird would have none of it. "My country is over here," he said. "Joseph is in the wrong direction, and why should I go to him?" Because, Baird answered, if the refugees went to Leavenworth, there was a good chance all would be returned to their country, but if they refused to go, there was little chance of anyone ever returning.

White Bird said, "I want to go back to my country, but will not go down to Leavenworth."

"Do any of you want to say anything?" Macleod asked the other Indians. "When White Bird spoke, he spoke for himself. Now I want to hear from the others."

"You know what I said," White Bird replied.

"Yes, you spoke for yourself. Now I want to hear from the others."

"What I said, I said for all my people."

But Macleod persisted: "What I want to know is whether you all agree with White Bird."

No-Hunter, the emissary that White Bird had wanted to send to Joseph, stood up. "As far back as I can remember," he said, whites and the Nez Perces had been friends. After reminding Baird of the aid the Nez Perces had given to the Americans in the Cayuse War of 1848, he observed:

> It seems that both parties, the white men and the Indians, don't want anymore trouble. As near as I can learn, my Indians and the Government don't want to fight against one another and now it seems there is a misunderstanding because White Bird does not want to surrender

and the Government does not want to send him back to his own country.

No-Hunter continued:

Now I see there is nothing to prevent my going to see Joseph. . . . I understand you to say that if I go it is no use going alone. I suppose if I go alone it won't cause a war between the Government and White Bird's band here. I know the feeling of the United States and the Canadian Governments and they want to treat the Indians kindly, so why can't I go down? . . . It won't take me long to go down and come back again, and I like to travel.

It was a reasonable petition, but Baird would not take the responsibility. He replied that his instructions did not allow for such a request: "All the letter [from department headquarters] was written for was because you wanted to surrender and we supposed you did want to."

Several Nez Perces asked, "Who is the man who came here and said we wanted to surrender?"

Irvine answered, "Henry, the young man who speaks English. He came and spoke to me in the camp about it."

One of the American scouts spoke up: "One of them told me if Joseph came over he would go."

Irvine interrupted, "I saw in the newspapers that three Nez Perces were coming up here, and I told the Indians so."

No-Hunter replied, "Henry ran away because his father is in Idaho. We did not know he wanted to go."

"Where is Joseph's daughter?" asked Baird.

"Henry knew he was lying, so he ran away. He took Joseph's daughter with him," No-Hunter answered.

"I did not know a word about it," interjected White Bird. "I was in another camp when they ran off."

It was obvious that a misunderstanding of some importance had occurred. The Mounted Police and the Americans were under the impression that the Nez Perce refugees wanted to surrender and return to the United States. Baird had arrived to collect them. But the Nez Perces assumed that Baird had come to negotiate, and acted accordingly. White Bird, No-Hunter, and the other Indians were not surrendering, they were negotiating, and they expected a response in kind.

Macleod tried to move the discussion back to the American proposals: "Have you made up your minds to accept the offer made you?"

Baird said, "I would not have come had I thought you did not intend to make friends with my government."

White Bird remained adamant about sending No-Hunter to see Joseph before the refugees made a decision. Baird and Macleod argued that the stories of the three Nez Perce emissaries were enough to convince the refugees of Joseph's good treatment—a hollow point, given Bald Head's statements. "You have only to look at those three men and see how happy they are," Macleod concluded.

No-Hunter was not convinced. "I would like to go and come back."

"Do you believe that those three men have been telling you lies?" Baird asked. "It is because you have seen them and I have no letter is the reasons I will not promise you will come back."

No-Hunter asked for time to think. With Macleod's permission, Baird replied, the Mounted Police would visit the Nez Perce camp, and those who wished to return with the Americans to the United States could bring their families and come to the fort for protection. Baird would wait for any who wished to come.

But when the police contingent returned that evening, only White Bird, No-Hunter, and a few warriors were with them. White Bird said, "We will not go." When Macleod asked if any of the others had anything to say, No-Hunter stated, "I will not go." Macleod tried one more time to persuade the refugees, but his arguments were met with silence. No-Hunter summed up: "Our chief does not want to go and we will not go either."[35]

Baird, his scouts, and the three Nez Perce emissaries returned to the United States, while White Bird and his people went back to their quiet but increasingly difficult lives on the plains near the Cypress Hills.

Gradually most of the remaining Nez Perce refugees made their way to the Lapwai reservation in Idaho, just as Henry did. Some were arrested by the authorities, and sent to join Joseph's people in Indian Territory. True to Baird's prediction, Joseph was not allowed to return to his country. He was sent to the hot flats of southern Kansas and, later, to a reservation in the state of Washington. Many of his people died.[36] Had Baird allowed No-Hunter to visit Joseph, the results of the conference probably would have been the same.

A few of the Nez Perces never returned to the United States. White Bird was one of them. Sometime in 1882 his skill as a shaman failed him and two Nez Perce children died of illness. Their irate father shot the headman dead.[37]

[35] Ibid. Here ends the account of "Monday Morning."

[36] Alvin Josephy, *The Nez Perce Indians and the Opening of the North West*, (New Haven, Ct.: Yale University Press, 1965), 619.

[37] Lucillius McWhorter, *Hear Me, My Chiefs!* (Caldwell, Id.: Caxton, 1952), 524.

CHAPTER 6

"...When There Are No More Buffalo or Game, I Will Send My Children to Hunt and Live on Prairie Mice..."

THE POLITICS OF HUNGER, 1878–1880

Although rumors of an alliance among the Northern Plains tribes in 1878 proved to be largely the invention of the citizens of Fort Benton, stories of an impending war continued to circulate through Montana and the Northwest Territories. The culprit was usually Sitting Bull, who allegedly darted around the region, hatching plots, forging agreements, acquiring weapons and supplies, and leading raids—a busy schedule. In June 1878, he reportedly led a party of warriors across the border and kidnapped the governor of Montana Territory from his sheep farm. The Sioux supposedly spirited the governor across the border, where Sitting Bull planned to hold him hostage for Chief Joseph's release. Some public embarrassment ensued when Gov. Benjamin F. Potts returned to Helena from his farm, unaware that he had been kidnapped and taken into the Canadian wilderness. But not even that episode softened widespread conviction that drastic measures were needed to avoid a crisis.[1]

[1] "Situation on the Dearborn," *Helena Herald*, 18 June 1878.

The citizens of Winnipeg were equally susceptible to rumors. Reports of the Cree revolt near Battleford that spring greatly upset the population, many of whom assumed that Sitting Bull had allied the Sioux with Big Bear and the Poundmaker. The *Manitoba Daily Free Press* reported that Canadian tribes were massing at the confluence of the Bow and Red Deer Rivers, and that Sitting Bull was organizing the Sioux, Nez Perce, Blackfeet, and mixed-bloods to attack Fort Macleod. To the editors of the *Press*, the situation was serious enough to merit abandoning their usual antipathy toward the Americans. If war broke out, they recommended that the U.S. Army be allowed to conduct a defensive campaign in the Northwest Territories, since the Mounted Police did not have adequate resources to counter such a threat.[2]

Within a week the alarm in Winnipeg evaporated. The Sioux, it was learned, had little to do with the Cree uprising, and no army of Plains Indians had descended on Fort Macleod. The *Press* observed that if the trouble with the Crees had actually resulted from the disappearance of the buffalo from the Northwest Territories, then the Sioux had contributed disproportionately to the problem. Sitting Bull would surely take advantage of the situation to construct a league against the whites.[3]

The inflated reputation of the Sioux refugees as marauders and conspirators inspired near-hysteria on both sides of the border. In the summer of 1878, a British couple was traveling with several guides on the plains west of Winnipeg. Algernon Heber Percy and his wife made their living sojourning in exotic places throughout the Empire and publishing accounts of their adventures. In the Northwest Territories they noticed a powerful climate of fear:

> We heard of Sitting Bull's Sioux being troublesome. Our horses stampeded in the night, what they were scared by I cannot say. Our men say a bear or a Sioux. All evil I notice is at once laid to the door of a bear or a Sioux.[4]

Several days later, the Percys' party

[2] "From the Far West! Threatened Indian Troubles! 'Our Guest' Sitting Bull Trying to Form a Grand Alliance!" *Manitoba Daily Free Press*, 20 March 1878, "Indian Difficulties in the North West," ibid., 23 March 1878.

[3] "Misunderstandings in the Far West," ibid., 26 March 1878; "What Consul Taylor Thinks About Sitting Bull," ibid., 29 March 1878.

[4] Algernon Heber Percy, *Journal of Two Excursions in the British North West Territory of North America* (Shropshire, England: Bennion and Horne, 1879), 8.

had an alarm of Sioux. Our horses first took fright, and after quieting them a wolf proceeded to make the night hideous with his singing. Now to imitate the howling of a wolf is the usual Sioux night signal, when they are mischief bent; and as our own men declared it was not Simon Pure who was singing, but a human imitation, we laid by our arms all night, very much on the quivive; however, nothing happened. With dawn, the wolf, for it was a wolf, moved off.[5]

The Percys and their guides made their way westward until they reached the Cypress Hills area, where they met the Sioux. The refugees seemed to be very hungry, the travelers observed, but "we are always much struck with the good manners and courtesy of the Indians."[6] The Percys and the Sioux shared some common opinions:

> We passed a Sioux camp, and went up to the lodges, where, after giving the usual present of tobacco, we had an animated conversation in signs, expressive of the mutual good-will of the English and the Sioux, and equal hatred of the Colonials, the Kitchimukoman, or Long Knives.[7]

The Percys concluded that the threat posed by the Sioux was overrated. The refugees did not like the Americans, but there was no evidence that they were preparing to invade Montana, or join the Crees in an alliance against the Dominion. The Percys' assessment was shared by an official of the Canadian Department of State who visited Fort Macleod and the Cypress Hills area in August. He found no evidence of plots or conspiracies, and told a correspondent of the *New York Times* that the rumors of a general war along the border were fantasies, or more likely distorted reports of the movements of hunting parties from reservations in the United States.[8] Similarly, several newspaper correspondents observed that nothing seemed to be happening in the region around Fort Walsh and Fort Macleod. Buffalo herds were very scarce, they noted, and a hard winter was predicted.[9]

Even so, the military districts of Montana and the Yellowstone "were held in readiness to take the field at short notice." By late summer, the army admitted that the Sioux refugees were not "swarming north of the Missouri River," but both district commanders received

---

[5] Ibid., 9.
[6] Ibid., 18.
[7] Ibid., 18–19.
[8] "Sitting Bull and His Comrades," *New York Times*, 4 August 1878.
[9] "Our Fort Walsh Letter," *New North-West*, 18 October 1878, "From Over the Border," 6 December 1878.

consistent reports of Indians in small parties ranging along the border. Col. John Gibbon concluded that the Sioux were simply hunting buffalo along the Milk and Marias rivers, since few of the animals were left in Canada. He did not regard them as a serious threat. But Nelson Miles saw menacing shadows along every hilltop and in every ravine, and once again bombarded department headquarters with alarming letters. Headquarters had grown used to this, and the decline in military activity continued despite the colonel's protests.[10]

The situation along the border was temporarily forgotten when violence broke out between whites and the Bannock Indians in the summer of 1878. After a series of skirmishes west across the Snake River plains and into central Oregon, the Bannocks were scattered and some escaped east through the mountains. There were fears that the Indians would flee across Montana and find sanctuary in Canada with the Sioux, and in fact many of them tried to do so. But they were cut off in Yellowstone National Park by Colonel Miles, who interrupted a vacation to lead a party of officers, enlisted men, and wives against them.[11] Although the colonel's tourists managed to maul the Bannocks and capture a few of the survivors, a small number of Indians eluded the cordon of troops in Montana and eventually crossed the border to join the camps of the Sioux.[12]

During the same period, a group of Northern Cheyennes broke out of internment on the southern plains and dashed toward the Powder River country or sanctuary in Canada. They were intercepted by the U.S. Army and imprisoned. Both the Bannock and Cheyenne outbreaks compelled British and Canadian authorities to resume watching events south of the border with care. Edward Thornton kept the Foreign Office in London closely informed of these events, and the Mounted Police contingents at Fort Walsh and Fort Macleod tracked down rumors and visited the refugee camps on a regular basis. In November, A. G. Irvine determined that some of the Bannocks were living in the Cypress Hills and Wood Mountain areas, but none of the Cheyennes had crossed the line.[13]

As the cold weather came on, the food situation steadily worsened in the Northwest Territories. By autumn there were scarcely any buffalo to be found north of the border, and toward the end of November the Mounted Police admitted that the Sioux were constantly sending hunting parties into Montana to find enough game to

---

[10] U.S. Secretary of War, *Annual Report, 1878*, "No. 3, Report of the Commanding General of the Department of the Dakota," 65–66.

[11] Ibid., "Report of Colonel Gibbon," 67.

[12] N.A.C., RG 7, file 2001, pt. 3d, "Macleod to R.W. Scott," 26 August 1878.

[13] Ibid., "Irvine to White," 24 November 1878.

survive. When Irvine rode into the camps that month, there were five hundred lodges of Oglalas, Hunkpapas, and Sans Arcs a few miles south of Wood Mountain. The refugees were undecided about what to do during the winter, and there was strong talk of moving the entire encampment into the United States to hunt buffalo along the Missouri River. "The women," Irvine wrote, "are urging the men to cross and save their children from starving."[14]

Sitting Bull led a small party across the border, and stayed for about a week, trading with Yanktons and Assiniboines from the Montana reservations. In return for skins and robes, the refugees received flour, corn, potatoes, and other foodstuffs. Later, the headman assured James Walsh that the Sioux would cross into the United States only to hunt and trade. But Sitting Bull believed that the situation would improve quickly, wrote Walsh, for "he was certain the Great Spirit would pity them and send the buffalo into the White Mother's country."[15]

By mid-December the food situation was very bad. A party of Nez Perces had visited a Crow camp south of the border, and White Bird told Sitting Bull that the Crows might join the exiled groups. The Crows had heard rumors that American soldiers were going to disarm them in the spring, and feared the consequences. Sitting Bull leaped at the opportunity. Abandoning his passive, pro-Canadian arguments, he declared in council that the Canadians and Americans were "fast friends" and the time was coming when the Mounted Police "would permit the Americans to cross the line and fight them." If the Sioux could convince the Crows and their own people on the Missouri River reservations to join them at Wood Mountain, they would be invulnerable to trickery or assault. The council agreed with Sitting Bull, and several days later a number of representatives were sent to the Crows and to meet with the reservation Sioux.

The emissaries returned without success. The reservation Sioux were not interested in the refugees' proposals; in fact former allies such as the Gros Ventres and Assiniboines at Fort Peck bitterly blamed the refugees for decimating buffalo herds and harassing their hunting parties.[16] The Crows had also refused Sitting Bull's proposal. Sitting Bull considered this a major insult and tried to organize a party of warriors to ride against the Crows on their reservation. On January 21, Walsh received word of the headman's plans and quickly set

[14] Ibid., 10 November 1878.
[15] Ibid., "Walsh to Irvine," 30 December 1878.
[16] U.S. Commissioner of Indian Affairs, *Annual Report, 1879*, "Blackfoot Agency, report of John Young, USIA," 195; ibid., "Fort Belknap Agency, report of W. L. Lincoln, USIA," 204; ibid., "Fort Peck Agency, report of N. S. Porter, USIA," 203.

out for Frenchman's Creek. Arriving two days later he "had a full view of the position of the camp, and also of the monuments marking the forty-ninth parallel"; the refugees had moved two and one-half miles south of the border. Technically, they were outside of Walsh's jurisdiction, but the police officer decided to pay the Indians an "informal" visit. Sitting Bull complained that the Americans had sent a Crow war party to Wood Mountain to steal Sioux horses, and asked what the Mounted Police would do about it. Walsh replied that there were too few Police to protect every camp, but that a complaint would be made to American authorities. He continued:

> I believe that you and the Nez Perces are to blame for this raid by the Crows. If you had not tried to plant sedition in the Crow tribe, by sending messengers to induce them to leave their reservations . . . the Crows would never have sent their young men into the White Mother's country.

"I never deny anything I do," Sitting Bull replied. The message had been sent to the Crows, he explained, because an alliance would make both tribes safe from the Americans:

> It was my wish to try to get every man that lived by the bow and arrow to confederate. . . . I wish to tell the White Mother that I will do to the Americans as they have done to me. It is not my wish to go to war, but I must.

Walsh answered that since Canada provided protection for the Sioux, there should be no reason to talk of alliances or war. He predicted that many of the refugees would oppose such policies, and noted that a number of Indians had already abandoned Sitting Bull's camp. But he failed to convince the headman.

Walsh's conversation with Sitting Bull soured the police officer, who had been sympathetic toward the Sioux. In a report to Irvine, he predicted that the Dominion would bear the blame for any trouble the Sioux might become involved in, "as we allowed [Sitting Bull] and his followers to recruit in strength, and to replenish their ammunition and arms." The Sioux hated not only the Americans, he told Irvine, but all whites, including Canadians. They showed this by their words and deeds, he claimed.[17]

Eroding goodwill among the Mounted Police posed a serious problem for the Sioux. The police had acted as a buffer between the Sioux and the governments of Canada, Great Britain, and the United States. They had shielded the refugees from politics and intrigue and had maintained security in the Wood Mountain area. Now, as the

[17] N.A.C., RG 7, file 2001, pt. 3d, "Walsh to Irvine," 25 January 1879.

field officers of the Mounted Police began to assume some of the attitudes of their superiors, the Indians' position in the Northwest Territories became increasingly tenuous. Both Irvine and Walsh recommended that the Sioux be handled quickly in an expedient way.

Walsh was correct in that the Americans did blame Canada for the activities of Indians who ranged through northern Montana that winter. These parties usually consisted of Canadian Blackfeet and Crees hunting buffalo near the Bear Paw Mountains. The disappearance of the large herds from the Northwest Territories blurred some of the political distinctions between the Sioux refugees and the Canadian tribes. In February 1879, the U.S. Department of State issued a complaint about border violations by Canadian Indians, the first in a series that would last until the mid-1890s.[18] But the Wood Mountain refugees remained the paramount American concern. In March, Secretary of State Evarts once again sent a note to Edward Thornton claiming that twenty-five hundred "armed and hostile" Sioux were camped on the border, hunting and raiding in Montana. Sitting Bull was fomenting alliances all over the northern plains, and the secretary demanded that the Dominion take all precautions necessary to prevent an "invasion" of United States territory.[19]

Evarts's persistence was matched by authorities in Ottawa, for different reasons. John A. Macdonald had replaced Alexander Mackenzie as prime minister, and he considered the growing instability in the Northwest Territories to be a high priority. In a letter to the minister of the interior, Macdonald surmised that the disappearance of the buffalo herds was causing severe competition between the tribes. At fault, the prime minister wrote, were "large numbers of foreign Indians at present within Canadian territory." According to Macdonald, the Sioux refugees were the most "troublesome." They were responsible for the agitation among the plains tribes by their "arrogance" and "actions," and by depleting the game resources of the Territories.

Macdonald believed that the buffalo herds in western Canada could not supply the tribes there for more than five years, after which the Dominion would be forced to feed and shelter its native populations. He predicted that depleted game resources would lead to increasing diplomatic problems between Canada and the United States, as more and more Indians crossed the border in search of food. Sitting

---

[18] Ibid., pt. 3a, "F. W. Seward, Acting Secretary, to E. Thornton," 13 February 1879. The last such event along the Montana-Canadian border was the deportation of five hundred Crees by the United States in the mid-1890s. The Crees were refugees of the North-West Rebellion of 1885.

[19] N.A.C., RG 7, file 2001, pt. 3d, "Evarts to Thornton," 15 March 1879.

Bull and his people would find ways to take advantage of the situation. To the prime minister, part of the solution seemed obvious: the Sioux must be returned to the United States. Macdonald's memorandum marked a stiffening in the Canadian government's attitude. Toleration gave way to harsher policies.[20]

Responding to renewed communications from the Canadian prime minister and the Marquis of Lorne, the new governor-general, the British government agreed to formally take up the issue with the United States. Sir M. E. Hicks-Beach, the colonial secretary, and Lord Salisbury, the foreign secretary, instructed Edward Thornton to present the Dominion's case to the U.S. Department of State once again. And once again, Secretary Evarts responded with a series of American complaints, this time about the border violations by Canadian Indians. He also submitted the well-worn claim that by granting the Sioux a refuge in the Northwest Territories, the Dominion had given them the status of "British Indians." Negotiations remained deadlocked.[21]

At the request of the Canadian Department of the Interior, A. G. Irvine traveled to Wood Mountain to warn the Sioux against using the Northwest Territories as a sanctuary from which to raid and hunt in the land of the "Queen's Allies."[22] Irvine found the Indians near the Mounted Police shack, preparing to move farther north to the Sand Hills area, where there was good fishing and reports of buffalo.[23] Irvine, too, had soured on the Sioux. The situation, he wrote, depended entirely upon the supply of game, and the refugees "have had buffalo all winter and have kept them back from our Indians who have had a hard winter and are all badly off." He predicted that starvation among the tribes in the next few winters would erode stability in the Territories and cause open violence.[24]

The refugees sensed that relations with the Mounted Police were foundering, for on March 20, Sitting Bull arrived at Fort Walsh with several members of his family and three other men. They had not eaten in several days, so Walsh gave them food and allowed them to camp in his front yard. The next day, several headmen from the Hunkpapa and Miniconjou groups in the area joined Sitting Bull, and together they met formally with Walsh. Sitting Bull was concerned about a report that an Indian named Black Wolf had told the

[20] Ibid., pt. 3a, "Macdonald to the Minister of the Interior," 28 February 1879.

[21] Ibid., "Lorne to Hicks-Beach," 10 March 1879, "Thornton to Lorne," 8 May 1879. See also U.S. House of Representatives, "Papers Relating to the Foreign Relations of the United States," 46th Cong., 2d sess., 1879, no. 217, 488–90.

[22] N.A.C., RG 7, file 2001, pt. 3a, "Lorne to Irvine," 24 March 1879.

[23] Ibid., "Irvine to Dennis," 4 May 1879.

[24] Ibid., "Irvine to Macleod," 23 April 1879.

agent at the Lower Yankton Agency that the refugees were ready to come back and wanted to negotiate with the American government. Black Wolf had no right to say this, Sitting Bull claimed:

> I have but one heart and it is the same today as when I first shook your hand, what I wish to say to the White Mother is, that when I first entered her country, I told you that my heart was pale at how my people had been persecuted by the Americans, and that I came to the White Mother's country to sleep sound and ask her to have pity [on] me—that I would never again shake the hand of an American.

He continued:

> I am looking to the north for my life, and hope the White Mother will never ask [me] to look to the country I left, although mine, and not even the dust of it did I sell, but the Americans can have it.
>
> Those who wish to return to the Americans can go, and those who wish to remain here, if the White Mother wishes to give them a piece of land, can farm, but I will remain what I am until I die, a hunter, and when there are no more Buffalo or game, I will send my children to hunt and live on prairie mice.

The refugees' horses were weak from the lack of forage, and could not be ridden far to find food. He did not want to violate "the laws of the Queen," Sitting Bull said, but he could not let his people starve. "You have for many months been advising us to think of getting our living from the ground," he said. "Will you tell me where we will find this ground?"

Walsh replied that there was no country superior to the Cypress Hills area, but the Indians would have an easier time on the American reservations, for there they would be supplied with seeds and tools, and taught how to farm. He was skeptical of the headman's intentions, and pointed out that barely two months before he had been plotting raids against the Crows. Not true, insisted Sitting Bull; he had simply been preparing to defend the refugees from an attack by the Crows and their American allies.

Walsh warned that game would get scarce, and within a few years not even the small herds in Montana would remain. The police officer had heard that a railroad would be built soon along the Missouri River, and that within a year a large U.S. military post would be constructed on the Milk River. Both projects would bring many Americans into the region, he predicted, and the Sioux would be hunted down if they crossed the border.[25]

[25] Ibid., "Walsh to Irvine," 25 March 1879.

That Sitting Bull would ask to be shown how to farm seems indicative of the refugees' desperate circumstances. Apparently, he was serious. In the spring his nephew, Watogola, petitioned the Canadian Department of the Interior for provisions, seeds, tools, and other farming implements. But the prime minister refused to consider the request, and the Privy Council agreed. The only alternative to starvation, the Canadian government implied, was for the refugees to return to the United States.[26]

Even surrender seemed impossible. U.S. Secretary of State Evarts sent a blistering letter to the British government complaining the Indians at the Fort Peck reservation "say that they find Uncpapas from Sitting Bull's camp everywhere, driving and scattering the buffalo and other game, and stealing their horses and running them over the boundary line." If something was not done to contain the refugees, Evarts warned, the United States would resort to armed force, even if it meant upsetting relations with Canada and Great Britain. The United States government demanded that the Dominion either repulse Indians who fled to the Northwest Territories to escape punishment for criminal acts, or disarm and intern them.

The Sioux, Evarts continued, "have, in the most formal manner possible to their savage state, renounced their rights in one country . . . to seek and receive asylum [and] residence in another." The secretary criticized Canadian authorities for giving "countenance" to the "assumption by which these savages may quit or resume allegiance or protection at will, by the mere circumstances of passing to the one side or the other of a conventional line traced through the wilderness." The Sioux had accepted British protection and authority, Evarts claimed, and no British or Canadian official had denied them that privilege. The United States government would henceforth regard the refugees as British Indians and the responsibility of Canada.[27]

This was no help at all. James Walsh might have explored the possibilities of agriculture with Sitting Bull, to convince him that sedentary farming in the Northwest Territories was preferable to starvation. The Dominion might have asked the United States government to share a substantial portion of the cost for land, relocation, provisions, equipment, and education. Canada would have taken a step toward stabilizing the situation in the Territories, and the United States government would have been rid of a group of Indians that it did not want. Sitting Bull and his people would not have had to return to the

[26] Ibid., "Copy of the Report of a Committee of the Hon. the Privy Council for Canada," 28 June 1879.

[27] Ibid., "Evarts to Thornton," 27 May 1879.

hated American reservations, nor succumb to hunger. But such compromises may have been impossible by 1879.

New sources of friction arose during the summer. Louis Riel, the Métis revolutionary, returned to the Northwest Territories after a long exile in Montana. Riel visited a camp of Métis traders near Wood Mountain, and reportedly had conversations with Sitting Bull and the other Sioux headmen. The refugees showed little interest in Riel's vision of nationhood for the Métis and the Indians in the Territories. Riel remained in the vicinity, however, making contacts and attempting to forge an alliance between the Métis and the various Canadian tribes.[28]

To the south, the Department of the Dakota headquarters ordered Colonel Miles to deploy his troops along the border to prevent hunting parties from crossing into the United States. During the winter, Miles had been in Washington serving on the Army Equipment Board. He had used the time to advocate an armed expedition into Canada to fight the Sioux, similar to Col. Ranald Mackenzie's 1873 campaign against the Kickapoos in Mexico. Sherman had finally had enough of Miles. Writing to Philip Sheridan, the general complained: "I have told him plainly that I know of no way to satisfy his ambitions but to surrender to him absolute power over the whole Army, with President & Congress thrown in." To Miles, Sherman wrote: "Because as you explained Generals Sheridan and Mackenzie once consented to act unlawfully in defiance of my authority in a certain political contingency is no reason why I should imitate so bad an example."[29]

Miles kept the Fifth Infantry and Second Cavalry operating all summer, as patrols weaved patterns back and forth between Fort Benton and the Fort Peck agency. Under Sherman's supervision, he conducted a cautious campaign. But when a correspondent of the *Chicago Times* asked him, "Supposing you have an engagement with Sitting Bull and whip him, will you respect the boundary line in case he should retreat across it?" Miles was noncommittal: "That must be an after consideration. I can hardly give a specific answer."[30]

As the summer wore on, Miles extended his operations to the Canadian line. On July 17, as Lt. William Philo Clark and a unit of Cheyenne and Sioux auxiliaries scouted a southern tributary of the Milk River, they ran across a party of hunters, reportedly led by

[28] Ibid., "Walsh to Irvine," n.d.

[29] Library of Congress, "William T. Sherman papers," "Sherman to Sheridan," 9 March 1879; ibid., "Sherman to Miles," 10 March 1879.

[30] John F. Finerty, *War Path and Bivouac* (Norman, Ok.: University of Oklahoma Press, 1956), 245.

Sitting Bull himself. The party fell back to the Milk River, and after holding until their families crossed, counterattacked. Miles and the main body of soldiers arrived a few hours later and dispersed the Sioux with artillery.

Miles followed the Indians north. On July 21, he and his forces reached the boundary of "Europe," as the American troops called the Dominion, and bivouacked by the marker cairns directly south of Wood Mountain. Two days later, James Walsh arrived at the camp to discuss the situation with the colonel. Miles complained about Canadian traders selling arms to the refugees, but Walsh remained adamant that "the Sioux don't want to fight white people anymore." Before an evening campfire, Walsh performed a pantomime of Spotted Eagle asking for peace, but his act failed to convince the American officers.[31]

Walsh left the camp with an American newspaper correspondent, John Finerty of the *Chicago Times*. They reached Sitting Bull's camp at Wood Mountain on July 30, and visited for several days while the Mounted Police met with the headmen. The results must have been familiar to all but Finerty. The Police warned the refugees against riding south of the border and the Sioux berated the Americans and protested their loyalty to the Queen and the Dominion. But Finerty noticed palpable signs of strain in the encampment. Arms and ammunition were plentiful, but food of any kind was scarce. Every day, the women wandered into the wooded bluffs to gather berries and pinenuts to supplement what little meat they had. Finerty noticed something else: from time to time the Mounted Police brought in wagonloads of food, a contravention of Dominion policy, courtesy of James Walsh.[32]

While Finerty visited the camp, a wounded man was carried in from the south. He had been hunting across the border when he and his party were set upon by Miles's scouts, and he had received a bullet in the lower abdomen. Barely had he been carried into a lodge when the man died. Afterward, the Sioux displayed a marked coolness toward the American correspondent, and Walsh advised Finerty to leave the following day.[33] On the trail back to Miles's camp, the correspondent and a Mounted Police escort were accosted by a group of Cheyenne scouts attached to the Fifth Infantry. As Finerty told it, only their last-minute recognition of the correspondent saved the American and the Canadians from being killed.

[31] Ibid., 264–66. See also, U.S. Secretary of War, *Annual Report, 1879,* 61–64.
[32] Finerty, *War Path and Bivouac,* 280–84.
[33] Ibid., 286–87.

Finerty returned to find the regiment packing to move south. Orders had come restricting Miles's operations to the south bank of the Missouri River, probably because the Canadian government had complained about reports that the colonel had sent agents and covert patrols across the border.[34] The withdrawal of the American troops left a vast region unpoliced, including the Belknap and Peck reservations. Barely had Miles pulled out when alarmed messages from the reservation agents reached the Office of Indian Affairs, stating that the Canadian Métis, the Sioux refugees, and groups of Crees were moving through the area, stealing food and driving off the buffalo.[35] Such was the severity of the food shortages in the Northwest Territories that when the army moved out of northern Montana, the Indians immediately moved in.

John Finerty was not the only American to visit the camps of the Sioux. Abbot Martin Marty returned to Wood Mountain to try to convince the refugees to come to the American reservations. This time he was confident he would succeed, because the threat of starvation was a powerful argument. Marty convinced the U.S. Army and the Canadian Department of the Interior to give him credentials, and in October 1879 he arrived at Fort Walsh on what he termed a "pastoral visit."[36]

After looking for the Sioux for twelve days, Marty and his Mounted Police guide found Spotted Eagle's camp along the banks of Frenchman's Creek, just north of the border. The abbot arranged to meet with other headmen in the area, but he did not invite Sitting Bull. It made little difference. Marty painted a bleak picture of starvation and disease in the Territories and contrasted it with the "bright optimism" on the American reservations, but the Sioux remained unmoved. Four speakers rose one after the other to reiterate their reasons for remaining in Canada. In a letter to the Canadian government, the abbot concluded the obvious: the Sioux did not like the Americans, and would not return. They could not accept the fact that the great buffalo herds of ten or twenty years before were gone. Spotted Eagle and the other headmen were confident that nature and the Great Spirit would provide for them. Only the disappearance of the last animal would convince them, Marty maintained.

Marty made two recommendations to the Canadian government. First, he called for British and Canadian authorities to demand "the

---

[34] Ibid., 236.

[35] N.A.C., RG 7, file 2001, pt. 3a, "N. S. Porter to O.I.A.," 25 October 1879.

[36] Ibid., "Campbell, memo.," 13 August 1879; ibid., "Marty to Dennis," 31 October 1879.

restoration of traditional, tacit understanding between the two Governments, by which the Indians on both sides of the International Line are allowed to follow the Buffalo wherever they go." Damages attributed to the Indians would be the responsibility of the individuals committing the act. Marty wanted to hold the Indians responsible to the laws of the United States and the Dominion of Canada, and subject to the privileges and penalties. There were serious problems with this idea, chief among them the inability of nomadic peoples to pay for damages, but at least the suggestion represented movement beyond the stalemate that had existed for more than two years.

Second, Marty proposed that the United States contribute the restitution agreed upon in treaty with the Sioux to the Canadian government, to fund land acquisition, education, and agricultural development for the refugees. The abbot claimed that relations between the United States and the refugees were similar to that of a debtor and a creditor. The Sioux were creditors for land taken by the United States, and therefore had the right to determine the time and place of payment from the debtor. The Dominion government took no action upon Marty's recommendations.[37]

During the winter, most of the refugees remained camped in between the Cypress Hills and Wood Mountain. James Walsh, burdened by years on the frontier, a dying father back East, and increasing displeasure among superiors who accused him of patronage toward the Sioux, was transferred from Fort Walsh to an eastern command. The new superintendent was L. N. F. Crozier, a strict career officer with little idealism or compassion toward Indians in the Northwest Territories. Crozier toured the district in February 1880 and found a deteriorating situation. During the winter, horse theft had brought tensions between various Canadian tribes and the Sioux refugees to a flash point. Stealing horses was no longer a game—the meat was the new staple of survival.[38]

As spring approached, Louis Riel renewed his activities in the region. He met with Sitting Bull and tried to persuade the headman to allow him to intercede with American authorities on his behalf. Riel advised Sitting Bull to "Keep the peace and do not get between two fires until Spring at any rate. If you want then to go back and live in peace with the Americans, I will see the President and arrange everything for you." Crozier suspected that Riel was trying to organize another rebellion.[39] But Sitting Bull was not interested in Riel's help, and the revolutionary soon left to concentrate on Métis and

[37] Ibid., "Marty to Dennis," 31 October 1879.
[38] Ibid., "Crozier to Dennis," 3 February 1880.
[39] Ibid., 22 February 1880.

Cree groups to the north and east of the Cypress Hills. As winter broke, conditions were alleviated to a small degree by warmer weather and better forage.

In May 1880, Edward Thornton met with William Evarts, and once again both men repeated a tired litany. After listening to demands that the Dominion disarm and intern the Sioux, the British minister replied that the Americans were responsible for the situation because they had forced their own Indians to take refuge in the Northwest Territories. Canada did not have the resources to disarm, intern, or feed the Sioux, nor would it be fair if the Dominion were forced to attempt such actions. Evarts argued that the fault lay in the fact that Great Britain possessed colonies in the Western Hemisphere. If the British "had the advantage of being a great nation," the secretary stated, they "also had its obligations." The meeting achieved nothing.[40]

The situation in the Northwest Territories could not continue much longer. The winter of 1881 would signal the end of traditional nomadic cultures on the Canadian plains. Dominion authorities were reinforcing the Mounted Police contingents to meet the anticipated disorder, and preparing to import bulk foodstuffs to feed the treaty Indians. The Sioux and their fellow refugees had managed to avoid starvation through foraging, adept hunting, and sometimes theft, but these measures would probably not suffice when the season turned cold again. The time had come to choose between starvation or surrender, but the situation had dragged on for so long that it had lost its sense of immediacy, and had become the subject of irritation or disinterest in Canada and the United States. The refugees were judged to be a fading danger, increasingly irrelevant to more pressing events in the Territories. Left alone on the plains without game or buffalo to hunt, the Sioux would be forced to make the draconian choice very soon.

---

[40] Ibid., "Thornton to the Earl of Granville," 10 May 1880.

CHAPTER 7

The Return of the
"Gall-Hearted Warriors"

THE SIOUX SURRENDER,
1880–1881

Starvation, stagnation, and fragmentation among the tribes brought on a pale imitation of peace. As the spring and summer of 1880 wore on, it became apparent that conditions had reached an equilibrium across the Northern Plains. The Canadian tribes were generally quiescent and withdrawn. Of the Sioux on the Rosebud, Pine Ridge, and Standing Rock reservations in the United States, the commissioner of Indian Affairs reported:

> Their behaviour has been orderly and peaceable during the year, and a fairer record could not reasonably be asked for from 14,000 wild, restless Indians, who four years ago, during the Sitting Bull campaign, furnished the largest number of recruits for the hostile ranks.[1]

Exhaustion and enforced domestication had prevailed.

[1] U.S. Commissioner of Indian Affairs, *Annual Report, 1880,* 104.

By mid-1880, troops of the Department of the Dakota had completed a series of telegraph lines across the length of Montana. The citizens of Fort Benton finally got their military post; a fort was built on the upper Milk River. Work on the Northern Pacific Railroad progressed as far as the Fort Peck reservation, and it was expected that the track would be laid to the passes of the Rocky Mountains by the spring of 1881.[2] The region looked less like the foreboding Big Dry of 1876 and more like the sparsely settled environs of the American Midwest. Peace had come to Montana, even if it was a peace of grinding defeat and poverty for some Indians.

The refugees at Wood Mountain and in the Cypress Hills area were relatively quiet, and spent most of their time trying to find food. That summer, hunting parties constantly crossed the border in search of buffalo and other game. Colonel Miles's soldiers spent a hectic season tracking them down, but could not engage them with any success.[3] Many of the Sioux had surrendered to the Americans during the winter. In January, forty-one families had appeared, destitute and hungry, at the Fort Peck agency, and gave their guns and horses to the agent. N. S. Porter had added them to the reservation rolls, but the trickle of returnees quickly developed into a flood. Families and small groups came into the agency throughout the spring and summer, eventually totalling 1116 people—109 men, 209 women, and 798 children. They had subsisted on their horses for several months, and suffered from malnutrition and disease. The men turned over a collection of antiquated weapons: forty muzzle loaders and broken breechloaders, and seven pistols.[4] More than a thousand Sioux surrendered to Miles's soldiers at Fort Keogh, after the colonel warned that he would "take to the field against them" if they did not come in.[5] As the solidarity of the Sioux crumbled, many made the choice between starvation and the reservation in defiance of Sitting Bull and his council.

As if to underscore this point, the agent at the Fort Belknap reservation, W. S. Lincoln, received an offer by several exiled headmen to surrender if an arrangement could be made with the United States

[2] U.S. Secretary of War, *Annual Report, 1880,* "Report of Brigadier-General A. Terry," 65–67.

[3] Ibid., 67. Miles would get his brigadier's star in December of 1880, and move on from Fort Keogh to command the Department of the Columbia.

[4] U.S. Commissioner of Indian Affairs, 1880, "Report of N. S. Porter," 235. The number of children in this group and the condition of the firearms they turned in suggest that these refugees were persons who could not survive any longer at Wood Mountain, and were sent south to surrender.

[5] U.S. Secretary of War, *Annual Report, 1880,* "Report of Brigadier-General A. Terry," 67.

government. The Office of Indian Affairs ordered Lincoln to "abstain from any communications," and "that ended the matter." Lincoln claimed to have received a pipe and a hatchet from Sitting Bull himself as a token of friendship, and was convinced that the intentions of the refugees were genuine.[6] But the Department of State still played a game with Her Majesty's government: Secretary of State William Evarts constantly sent complaints and demands to the British Legation, as if repetition could achieve what diplomacy had not.[7]

Sitting Bull apparently counted upon the intercession of James Walsh, who had promised the headman before his departure that he would try to take the refugees' case before Prime Minister Macdonald in Ottawa and before President Hayes in Washington. Macdonald agreed to meet with Walsh, but remained convinced that the best policy was to wait until starvation forced the Sioux to return to the United States. The prime minister refused to permit Walsh to present his case to the Hayes administration in an official capacity. The police officer was ordered to take up a new position in Qu'Appelle immediately. The Sioux remained in limbo, caught in the conflict between three governments.[8]

At about the same time that Walsh was pleading the refugees' case in Ottawa, Edwin H. Allison, an American scout and interpreter, appeared in the Wood Mountain area. Allison had formerly been in the employ of the owners of the "Circle F" ranch in the Sun River range of Montana. He claimed to have been hired at Fort Belknap as an interpreter to the Sioux by J. R. Cox and William Floweree, two ranchers who were driving twelve hundred head of cattle from the upper Milk River to the railhead at Bismarck, North Dakota. The ranchers decided to take the cattle through the heart of the Sioux range because of the abundance of forage, wood, and water, and Allison was brought along in case of encounters with the Indians.[9]

On August 1, 1880, the cattle drive reached the confluence of the Milk River and Frenchman's Creek, and Allison had the opportunity to work for his wages. The outfit ran into a large hunting party led by the headman Gall, who had known Allison for many years.

[6] U.S. Commissioner of Indian Affairs, *Annual Report, 1880*, "Report of W. S. Lincoln," 238.

[7] U.S. House of Representatives, "Papers Relating to the Foreign Relations of the United States, 1880" (Washington, D.C., Government Printing Office: 1880), 497–98, 507–8.

[8] N.A.C., RG 7, file 2001, pt. 3d, "Dewdney to Macdonald," 23 October 1880.

[9] Edwin H. Allison, *The Surrender of Sitting Bull* (Columbus, Oh.: Walker Lithograph and Printing, 1891), 9–10. Allison's account is self-serving, but there is little doubt that his relationship with Gall was instrumental in conducting negotiations with the Sioux.

Even so, the interpreter took no chances. He told the headman that the cattle were bound for Canada, because "they belonged to the Queen of England," and had been purchased for the larders of the Mounted Police. With that, the encounter became very friendly, for, as Allison put it: "I hardly think the Gall believed my story, but it might be true, and . . . it would not do to molest persons or property under the protection of the British government."[10] Allison invited Gall and several other Indians to dine with the ranchers on steak that evening, and everything went well.

During the feast and the discussion that followed, Allison concocted the idea of visiting Sitting Bull in Canada and convincing him to surrender. Gall would give no promises, but he appeared mildly encouraging and even told the interpreter the location of the main Sioux encampment—at "Ruined Timber," a stretch of forested hills twenty miles north of Wood Mountain, near a trading post and a small garrison of Mounted Police. The headman invited Allison to come for a "visit."

Allison recognized his chance for glory. As soon as the drive reached Fort Buford he presented himself to the commanding officer, who recognized that there might be enough glory for two people in such a mission. Maj. David Brotherton authorized Allison's proposal by hiring him as a scout for the army and allowing him to draw on military stores for the supplies he needed. Four days after leaving the fort, Allison sat on the crest of Wood Mountain as the sun went down, scanning the northern ridges with a pair of binoculars. In a draw between two spurs of the mountain he sighted a thick haze—the sign of many campfires. Gall openly welcomed Allison to the refugees' principal camp. The scout stayed for three days, but did not see Sitting Bull. Before he left, he extracted a promise from Gall to meet again on the Missouri River in twenty-two days to discuss terms of surrender.[11]

Allison returned to Fort Buford to find Brotherton in a foul mood; the major had been dressed down by General Terry for authorizing the scheme. But the scout's report changed Terry's mind, and the department commander gave permission for a second mission to the refugees, this time with a wagonload of provisions to use as an enticement. Allison set out for the rendezvous immediately with a volunteer enlisted soldier named Day.

On October 25, Allison and Day met a messenger from Gall, who told them that the refugees could be found on the American side of the border, near the confluence of Frenchman's Creek and

[10] Ibid., 13, 14.
[11] Ibid., 22–26.

the Milk River. When Allison reached the camp, the Indians told him that he would be a guest of Sitting Bull in the headman's lodge, for as long as he stayed. The scout complied, puzzled by the headman's gesture, and after a friendly meal with Sitting Bull, he sought out Gall. From him, Allison learned of a political struggle of major proportions among the refugees: Gall meant to surrender everyone, "Sitting Bull and all," but honor demanded that certain promises be discharged first. To avoid the stigma of surrender and an open clash with Sitting Bull, Gall would first encourage the headman to visit James Walsh at Fort Walsh, for the Sioux expected the police officer to come there soon. Gall proposed to rendezvous with Allison afterward at Wood Mountain. But Allison demanded a show of faith to ensure the army's continued confidence in him. The headman offered to send twenty families to Fort Buford as a gesture of good will, "but he cautioned me not to let Sitting Bull know of their real purpose, but to lead him to suppose they were only going into the Agency on a visit to their friends."[12]

Allison had no problems with the plan; he told Gall that he did not care for Sitting Bull. After the Canadian government had rejected his offer to compromise, Sitting Bull had become entrenched in old dreams and strategies that no longer applied to the situation. He was determined to wait for Walsh to intercede for the Sioux, and he did not understand that there was nothing more that the superintendent could do for him. Events had escaped his grasp, and he was slowly being stripped of influence. In his place others had stepped in who were more adaptable, or perhaps merely tired of inaction. Gall was the most reputable headman among the dwindling groups of refugees. While Sitting Bull waited, Gall moved carefully, out of deference for the older man's enormous reputation. Allison believed that Gall now made the decisions and assumed daily administrative responsibilities; Sitting Bull had become a figurehead.[13]

Gall made good on his promise. When Allison and Day set out for Fort Buford the next day, they found twenty families waiting for them near Poplar Creek. The scout brought them in and remained at the post for five days before leaving for Wood Mountain. Disturbing news awaited Allison when he reached Fort Peck. Partisans of Sitting Bull had discovered what Gall was up to, and accused him of instigating the desertion of twenty lodges at Allison's behest. When confronted by Sitting Bull,

[12] Ibid., 36.
[13] Allison stated that he negotiated a surrender only with Gall. His conversations with Sitting Bull did not broach the subject.

and concealment being no longer possible, Chief Gall, characteristically prompt in action, had leaped into the midst of camp, and publicly called upon all who acknowledged him as their Chief, to separate themselves from the followers of Sitting Bull, and prepare immediately to follow him to Fort Buford.[14]

Three hundred lodges, roughly half of the camp, had pulled out with Gall that night and arrived at Fort Peck on November 25. Allison was still determined to convince Sitting Bull to come in. After arranging for Gall and his people to remain at the agency until his return, the scout rode toward the border. He found the remaining refugees near Wood Mountain. L. N. F. Crozier of the Mounted Police was visiting the camp, and he arranged for Allison and Sitting Bull to meet at a nearby trading post that evening.

Over dinner, the meeting showed promise. Although Allison did not like Sitting Bull—he was, the scout later wrote, "constitutionally a coward"—he did feel sympathy for the headman, reduced to tears over the "distressed, hunted condition" of his people and the "hopelessness of their children's future."[15] Allison emphasized those fears as eloquently and forcefully as he could over the next few days. On December 11, with Crozier's help, he extracted a promise from Sitting bull to surrender. The next morning the entire camp set out toward the Missouri River, while Allison circulated among the Indians with encouraging words.[16]

Starvation had affected the refugees' health and their horses' endurance, so progress was slow. They reached the confluence of the Milk and Missouri rivers within two days, where they had the luck to run across a large herd of buffalo. The Sioux paused and hunted for a few days, and with their supplies replenished, there was serious talk of retracting their promise to surrender. After a long argument, the scout managed to convince Sitting Bull to send three volunteers to Fort Buford to judge for themselves whether the Americans were sincere. But no one wanted to volunteer. "For a long time there was no response. Finally, after the assembled warriors had smoked their pipes in silence for twenty minutes, causing a feeling of portentous gloom to pervade the atmosphere," a man named Patriarch Crow arose. He reminded the others that since warriors "were never lacking for deeds in war, neither shall they be lacking when called for a mission of peace." He sat down by Allison's side. Patriarch Crow's anxiety was palpable; Allison noticed "great drops of

---

[14] Allison, *Surrender of Sitting Bull*, 50.
[15] Ibid., 53–55.
[16] Ibid., 63–66.

sweat rolling off his face" in the cold damp of the council place. But the impasse was broken and two other Indians soon volunteered. Allison and his party left for Fort Buford the next morning.[17]

The group arrived at the fort on Christmas Eve, 1880. They stayed for several days while arrangements were made for the returning Sioux, and the soldiers tried to convince Sitting Bull's representatives of the Americans' sincere intentions. On the way back to Sitting Bull's camp, Allison detoured to Fort Peck to visit Gall.

Since the Fort Peck agency would be the focal point of surrender, General Terry had ordered Maj. Guido Ilges and five companies to reinforce the garrison at Poplar Creek. Ilges arrived with an indelicate attitude, considering the cautious character of negotiations up until that point. When the major interviewed Gall, he demanded that the headman surrender his people immediately and prepare to move to Fort Buford in a few days. Gall reiterated his willingness to surrender, but observed that the weather was very severe and asked if the Sioux might stay at the agency until the cold let up or Allison returned. But Ilges insisted. The interview deteriorated into a shouting match, as both Ilges and Gall threatened one another.[18]

Ilges ordered an assault upon the Sioux encampment at noon on December 31. Barely twenty minutes after the first shots were fired, a white flag appeared, carried by Gall himself. The headman quickly surrendered to Ilges, and managed to keep his people from fleeing while the soldiers disarmed them. Eight Indians were killed in the fight. The soldiers had suffered no casualties.[19]

Allison, who had arrived at the agency in time to witness the attack, was enraged. He regarded Ilges' impatient actions as an attempt to grab some glory, and he realized that he could not leave Fort Peck until the situation stabilized. During the battle, the scout had noticed several of Gall's warriors riding westward up the Missouri River toward Sitting Bull's camp. Fearful that the Indians would tell Sitting Bull about a massacre, Allison asked Patriarch Crow to go and try to convince the refugees of the Americans' good intentions.

[17] Ibid., 68–70.
[18] Ibid., 73–76. See also, U.S. Secretary of War, *Annual Report, 1880*, "Report of Brigadier-General A. Terry," 100–107.
[19] Allison, *Surrender of Sitting Bull*, 73–76. Ilges' account of the engagement differs from Allison's. The major characterized the mood of the refugees as bellicose and dangerous, and defended his actions. Allison disagreed: "[Major Ilges] reached Camp Poplar Creek before me, and immediately undertook a little work on his own account, and for his own glory, which, only for the prompt and decided action, first, of Chief Gall . . . would have undone all the work I had thus far accomplished" (p. 72). General Terry's report to the secretary of war was inconsistent with either account, and treated Ilges's actions in an ambiguous manner (U.S. Secretary of War, *Annual Report, 1880*, 100–107).

When Patriarch Crow reached Sitting Bull's camp, the refugees were packing up to move back into the Northwest Territories. He managed to shame them into halting their preparations, and that evening he told them of his treatment at Fort Buford. But ambition got the better of Patriarch Crow, and the next morning he openly challenged Sitting Bull. He compelled the headman to move his lodge to a small clearing in the timber a few hundred yards from the camp, and he "called on all who were cowards, to remove their tepees to the opening with Sitting Bull, but those who were not cowards should remain where they were." Forty-three families joined the headman in the clearing, but about three hundred remained with Patriarch Crow, who told Sitting Bull to leave and not stop until he had crossed the Canadian border. Sitting Bull "went, and soon disappeared in the wind driven snows of the north."[20]

Under the circumstances, Allison could hardly have hoped for more. On February 10, 1881, he returned to Fort Buford with over six hundred lodges of refugees. Only Sitting Bull and a few of the Sioux remained out, and Allison concluded that the headman "was left without a following, and his power . . . being entirely destroyed, it was a matter of indifference to our government if he himself never came in."[21]

In late January, Sitting Bull and about fifty lodges of Indians camped at Wood Mountain. There the headman waited for James Walsh to return. When spring came and Walsh did not show up, Sitting Bull rode to Qu'Appelle to find him. Instead, A. G. Irvine and Edgar Dewdney, the Canadian commissioner of Indian Affairs, met the headman and told him that the Dominion could not help his people. A reserve of land would not be set aside for the scattering of refugees left in the Northwest Territories, nor would supplies be made available. Irvine told Sitting Bull not to wait for Walsh; he would not come.

The message was consistent with the hardening views of the government in Ottawa. The food crisis expected in the fall of 1881 left Dominion authorities with little inclination to deal with the Sioux. During the last months of the Hayes administration, U.S. Secretary of State William Evarts initiated yet another round of discussions regarding the refugees. Again he met with Edward Thornton, this time stating that two years of "predatory incursions" were too much for the United States government to bear, and he demanded that Great Britain fulfill "its obligations of neighborly courtesy and good

---

[20] Allison, *Surrender of Sitting Bull*, 82–83.
[21] Ibid., 84.

will," and intern the Sioux.[22] But Canada refused, and pointed out that its policies had resulted in the surrender of the majority of the refugees without bloodshed. Officials in Ottawa had recommended to the Privy Council that the best course was to discourage the United States government from making threats and frightening the Indians, "leaving hunger to do its work."[23]

Sitting Bull returned to Wood Mountain to find that hunger and deprivation had become the rule. After a few weeks his determination appeared to waver, and he indicated that he might be willing to surrender. The offer was forwarded by the Dominion authorities to the U.S. Department of State. Maj. David Brotherton at Fort Buford was instructed to reopen negotiations with the refugees.[24] Edwin Allison was unavailable, so Brotherton solicited the services of Jean Louis Legare, a French-Canadian trader and territorial justice of the peace who had been dealing with the Sioux for nearly four years. But when Legare arrived at the camps of the Sioux, Sitting Bull had again changed his mind. The headman refused to give up, despite the fact that many of his followers were ready to surrender, including his daughter. Legare brought eighty refugees into Fort Buford in May of 1881 and then returned to Wood Mountain to meet with Sitting Bull a second time.[25]

For a couple of weeks the headman vacillated. In early July, hungry and beguiled by Legare's persistence, he relented. The trader quickly organized a train of wagons, hired Métis acquaintances as drovers, and moved the headman and his small group out on July 11. Brotherton sent two wagonloads of food to intercept the column, and instructed the officer in charge to assure the refugees that "they will be well treated here, and they need fear nothing in coming in." Artfully, carefully, Legare and Capt. Walter Clifford coaxed the refugees over the last hundred miles.[26]

On July 19, Sitting Bull entered Fort Buford and surrendered himself to Major Brotherton. Behind him crowded the remnants of the Great Sioux Confederacy—two hundred ragged, emaciated, frightened people, blinking in the sunlight and staring at the ground. They remained at the fort for ten days, and then were loaded onto a steamer

[22] N.A.C., RG 7, file 2001, pt. 3d, "Evarts to Thornton," 5 February 1881.

[23] Ibid., "Confidential Memorandum on the Subject of the Sioux Indians for the Consideration of the Hon. Privy Council," n.d.

[24] Ibid., "Lorne to Thornton," 26 April 1881. See also, "Report No. 277, Jean Louis Legare," House of Representatives, 51st Cong., 1st sess., 1890, 1–2. See also N.A.R.A., RG 123, Records of the United States Court of Claims, file C.J. no/15713, "Case of Jean Louis Legare."

[25] "Jean Louis Legare," HR Report No. 277, 1–2.

[26] Ibid., 3.

and taken down the Missouri to Fort Randall, where they were interned as "prisoners of war."[27] With their passing, one writer waxed:

> Instead of hearing the oft-heard war-whoop and murderous yells of the hideous savages on the battle-field and the retort of our Gatling guns and musketry, and the loud cheering of our brave boys in blue, you will hear the persuasive eloquence of the kind-hearted theologian and the knightly young schoolmaster, pleading the cause of Christianity and education; and where Sitting Bull oft-times held his medicine lodges and war dances on the banks of [the rivers], for no other purpose only to strengthen and bolster up the hearts of hundreds of Gall-hearted warriors, and urge them on to cold-blooded, heart-rending and blood-thirsty murders, you will see stately courthouses, with their benches occupied by the ablest jurists in the land to mete out justice, and members of the bar ably advocating and defending the cause of peace and good order.[28]

But Christianity, education, justice, peace, and good order paid an unnecessary price in this affair; if commentators of the day could find these, history cannot.

[27] U.S. Secretary of War, *Annual Report, 1881*, "Report of General Alfred Terry," 107–8.

[28] Judson Elliott Walker, *Campaigns of General Custer in the North-West and the Final Surrender of Sitting Bull* (New York: Argonaut Press Reprint, 1966), 111–12.

E P I L O G U E

In 1876, as the Sioux crossed the border into the Northwest Territories, a telegraph line was completed between Winnipeg and Battleford. During the following year, the rails of the Canadian Pacific Railroad reached across the Canadian Shield to the plains of Manitoba. By the summer of 1883, the rails extended through Calgary to the slopes of the Rocky Mountains.

As Canadian tribes were relocated onto the new reserves, the Mounted Police began to reassign their forces to posts along the railroad. In 1882, a year after Sitting Bull returned to the United States, Police headquarters was moved from Fort Walsh to a new facility on the outskirts of present-day Regina. A railroad through western Canada gave Ottawa the same benefits that the railroads south of the border gave to the United States government: military forces could be rapidly shifted across the frontier to meet developing crises. The Canadian Pacific line also brought surveyors and settlers to the Territories, and the Métis, led by Gabriel Dumont and Louis Riel, rebelled in 1885. The Cree Indians under the headman Big Bear joined them.

By the time of the rebellion, James Macleod had been replaced by A. G. Irvine as commissioner of the Mounted Police. The Canadian government directed Irvine to take a substantial force north to the Battleford area to control the situation, but hostilities broke out when the Police contingent drew near. At Duck Lake in late March, fifty-six Police officers and forty-three volunteers clashed with several hundred Métis and Indians. The Police retreated, leaving twelve of their own dead.

Ottawa had already ordered the mobilization of the Canadian militia, and within a few days an army was rolling west aboard special trains. After several indecisive engagements, the Métis-Indian coalition was shattered at Batoche in May. Riel was captured and later hanged. In the years following the rebellion, the Mounted Police extended their operations into the northern taiga and concentrated on enforcing the law in sparsely settled areas. As populations increased and districts were organized, the Police gradually gave up a number of their extraordinary civil responsibilities.

James Walsh retired from the force after several years at Qu'Appelle and other assignments in the East. In 1897, the Canadian government responded to problems created by a gold strike near the Alaskan border by appointing Walsh commissioner and chief executive of the Yukon District. One of his supporters was David Mills, who had remained in government as an influential member of Parliament. Walsh was given his old rank of Police superintendent and placed in charge of the contingent of officers in his district. He reported directly to the minister of the interior, while other Police superintendents were responsible to the commissioner of the force.[1]

Even after Sitting Bull returned to the United States, some of the Sioux refugees remained in Canada. By 1882, this small group had encamped near Moose Jaw, Saskatchewan, under a minor headman named Black Bull. In 1913, as a result of a campaign by a Presbyterian clergyman, A. D. Pringle, the Canadian Department of Indian Affairs gave these Indians a small reserve at Wood Mountain.[2]

In the United States, the surrender of Sitting Bull marked an end to an epoch. The nature of conflict between whites and Native Americans changed: rarely was a war fought in unorganized territories beyond a defined frontier. Violence, when it occurred, usually erupted on the reservations or on settled lands nearby, as Indians resisted white incursions onto their properties, or into their traditional culture. The white agenda in the 1880s was embodied in the Dawes Act: control and assimilation.

Gall settled on the Standing Rock reservation and befriended the agent in charge, James McLaughlin. The Sioux headman supported federal plans to educate Indian children, and in 1889 was appointed a judge on the Court of Indian Offenses at the agency. He remained bitterly against Sitting Bull, and quietly opposed the Ghost Dance religion in 1890. He died four years later, reportedly from an overdose of drugs.

Sitting Bull remained in confinement at Fort Randall until 1883, when he was allowed to go to Standing Rock. In 1885 he toured with William F. Cody in Buffalo Bill's Wild West show. He maintained prestige and power among his people, in part because of his unwavering opposition to the steady erosion of Sioux culture. Because of Sitting Bull's influence, Agent McLaughlin ordered him to be arrested during the Ghost Dance movement in 1890. When the tribal police

[1] R. G. Macleod, *The North-West Mounted Police and Law Enforcement, 1872–1905* (Toronto: University of Toronto Press, 1976), 81.

[2] George F. G. Stanley, "Displaced Red Men: The Sioux in Canada," *in* A. L. Getty and Donald B. Smith, eds., *One Century Later: Western Canadian Reserve Indians Since Treaty 7* (Vancouver, B.C.:1978), 68.

attempted to carry out the order on December 15, a fight broke out, and Sitting Bull, his son, and six of his bodyguards were killed.

Nelson Miles received a brigadier's star in 1880, and was in command of the Department of the Columbia when Sitting Bull surrendered. Later, he replaced George Crook in Arizona, where he negotiated the Apache headman Geronimo's surrender and then exiled him to Florida along with the Apache scouts who had helped to find him. Miles was in command of the Department of the Missouri when the Ghost Dance movement began. He ordered the arrest of both Sitting Bull and Big Foot, precipitating their deaths and the massacre at Wounded Knee. Miles characterized the massacre as an outrageous blunder, and criticized the officer commanding the Seventh Cavalry for incompetence. He also agitated for a national policy to disarm reservation Indians.

In 1894, Miles led veteran frontier troops into Chicago to quell rioting during the Pullman labor strike. A year later he was made General of the Army. Miles entertained ambitions about the presidency, and wrote two popular autobiographies toward that end, but few in the Republican party took his candidacy seriously. During the Spanish-American War, a public quarrel with the secretary of war prevented him from commanding the expedition to Cuba, but he did lead a successful campaign against minor Spanish resistance in Puerto Rico. Miles did not get along with Theodore Roosevelt—the president described him as "a vain peacock"—and he retired in 1903. Miles died of a heart attack while at the Ringling Brothers Circus in 1925, reportedly while standing at attention during the playing of the National Anthem.[3]

Relations between Canada, Great Britain, and the United States remained volatile until the First World War. During the 1880s a controversy over fishing rights and pelagic sealing arose, and a modus vivendi between Great Britain and the United States was derailed when the British minister in Washington expressed a preference for President Grover Cleveland over his Republican opponent in the election of 1888. Cleveland, partly tainted by a pro-British reputation, was defeated. American seizures of Canadian sealing ships continued until 1892, when the issue was submitted to international arbitration and settled.

Relations reached a nadir in 1895, when the United States demanded that a dispute between Great Britain and Venezuela over the boundary of the British colony of Guiana be submitted to arbitration. After months of delay the British government rejected the

[3] Virginia W. Johnson, *The Unregimented General: A Biography of Nelson A. Miles* (Boston: Houghton-Mifflin, 1962), 363.

demand, and Grover Cleveland, then in his second term, threatened war. Opposition quickly mounted from American and British intellectuals, businessmen, and farmers who had finally discovered their important economic and cultural ties. Canadian officials in Ottawa also expressed deep concern about the possibilities of conflict. Public sentiment forced both governments to agree not only to arbitrate the Venezuela-Guiana dispute but also to negotiate a treaty to cover future Anglo-American problems. In 1896, a dispute arose between Canada and the United States over the boundary line along the Alaskan panhandle. The Americans got what they wanted in 1903, when President Theodore Roosevelt managed to "stack" a tribunal appointed to decide the issue. British representatives effectively backed the position of the United States government.

The stage was set for an Anglo-American rapprochement that began in the late 1890s. American annexation of Canada was no longer considered a threat, and the United States presence in Asia and Latin America did not pose insurmountable problems for British foreign policy. The rise of Germany, Japan, and Russia caused anxiety in Great Britain, and the British government began to view the United States as an effective counterbalance in terms of trade and strategic considerations. In America, things British came into vogue, as ethnic and economic elites in the urban, industrializing areas of the East emphasized a shared Anglo heritage. The Atlantic partnership forged before and during the First World War was to last throughout the twentieth century.

In the larger context, the hegira of the Sioux refugees at Wood Mountain represented one of many final acts in an era that was fast drawing to a close. In Canada, the government brought the Northwest Territories under control, and the experiment of the Dominion would prove to be successful. In the United States the concerns of continental expansion under an agrarian aegis would soon be replaced by concerns of industry, urban culture, economic expansion, internationalism, and even national security. The rails and telegraph lines being laid across Montana in 1881 did not merely delineate a new era in the American West; they were, in a small way, harbingers of an outward-turning and refocusing of interests that would mark America in the twentieth century.

BIBLIOGRAPHY

A. Newspapers

Benton Record (Fort Benton, Montana), 1874–1881.
Chicago Times, 1878–1880.
Helena Herald, 1875–1881.
Manitoba Daily Free Press (Winnipeg, Manitoba), 1874–1881.
National Republican (Washington, D.C.), 1876–1878.
New North-West (Deer Lodge, Montana), 1876–1880.
New York Herald, 1876–1879.
New York Times, 1876–1881.
New York Tribune, 1876–1879.
New York World, 1876–1877, 1880.
Toronto Globe, 1876–1879, 1881.

B. United States Government Documents

U.S. Board of Indian Commissioners. *The Administration of Indian Affairs in Canada: Report of an Investigation Made in 1914* [by Frederick Abbott, Secretary of the BIC]. Washington, D.C., 1915.

U.S. Commissioner of Indian Affairs. *Annual Reports, 1876–1886.*

U.S. Congress. *Congressional Record*, 44th–46th Cong. (1876–1880).

U.S. Executive Documents. *Report of the Commission Appointed by the Direction of the President of the United States under Instructions of the Honorables Secretary of War and the Secretary of Interior, to Meet the Sioux Chief, Sitting Bull.* Washington, D.C.: GPO, 1877. [Also found in U.S. Commissioner of Indian Affairs. *Annual Report, 1877*, 718–23.]

U.S. Department of State. *The Case of the United States, to be Laid before the Tribunal of Arbitration, to be Convened at Geneva. . . . Washington, D.C.: GPO, 1872.*

————. *Reports upon the Survey of the Boundary between the Territory of the United States and the Possessions of Great Britain. . . .* Washington, D.C.: GPO, 1878.

U.S. House of Representatives. "Jean Louis Legare, Report," Report No. 277, 51st Cong., 1st sess., 1890.

————. "Jean Louis Legare, Adverse Report," Report No. 841, 53rd Cong., 2d sess., 1894.

————. "Papers Relating to the Foreign Relations of the United States," Executive Document 1, part 1, 45th Cong., 3rd sess., 1878.

————. "Papers Relating to the Foreign Relations of the United States," Executive Document 1, part 1, 46th Cong., 2d sess., 1879.

_____ . "Papers Relating to the Foreign Relations of the United States," Executive Document 1, part 1, 46th Cong., 3d sess., 1880.

_____ . "Papers Relating to the Foreign Relations of the United States," Executive Document 1, part 1, 47th Cong., 1st sess., 1881.

_____ . "Papers Relating to the Foreign Relations of the United States," Executive Document 1, part 1, 47th Cong., 2d sess., 1882.

_____ . "Papers Relating to the Foreign Relations of the United States," Executive Document 1, part 1, 48th Cong., 1st sess., 1883.

U.S. Senate. "Report to Accompany Amendment of Mr. Carter to H.R. 8293," Report No. 821, 54th Cong., 1st sess., 1896.

United States Reporter, "Cherokee Nation v. Georgia," 30–1.

_____ . "United States v. Joseph," 94.

C. Dominion of Canada Government Documents

Dominion of Canada, House of Commons. *Sessional Papers, Reports of the Department of the Interior, 1879–1881.*

_____ . *Annual Reports of the North-West Mounted Police, 1876–1881.*

D. Manuscript Collections

Glenbow Museum Archives, Calgary, Alberta. Anonymous Letter to "Cora" [daughter of James M. Walsh], May 21, 1890, file M3636.

Library of Congress, Washington, D.C., William T. Sherman papers.

National Archives of Canada. Record Group 7, Records of the Governor-General's Office, vols. 318–19, file 2001, parts 3a–3d.

_____ . Record Group 18, Records of the Royal Canadian Mounted Police, correspondence and subject files of the Commissioner's Office, 1876–1881.

National Archives and Records Administration. Record Group 59, Records of the Department of State, file T–24 10–9–5, consular records, "James W. Taylor correspondence."

_____ . Record Group 123, Records of the United States Court of Claims, file C.J. NO/15713, "Case of Jean Louis Legare."

_____ . Record Group 393, Records of the United States Army Continental Commands, District of Montana 1876–1886, "Letters and Telegrams Received," 1876–1881.

_____ . Record Group 393, Records of the United States Army Continental Commands, District of the Yellowstone and Yellowstone Command, 1876–1881, "Letters and Telegrams Received," 1876–1881.

_____ . Record Group 393, Records of the United States Army Continental Commands, District of the Yellowstone and Yellowstone Command, 1876–1881, "Letters and Telegrams Sent," 1876–1881.

E. Articles

Baird, George W. "General Miles' Indian Campaigns." *Century Magazine* 42 (1891): 351–70.

Gray, John S., ed. "Sitting Bull Strikes the Glendive Supply Trains." *Westerners Brand Book* 28 (1971): 25–27, 31–32.

Joyner, Christopher C. "The Hegira of Sitting Bull to Canada: Diplomatic Realpolitik, 1876–1881." *Journal of the West* 13 (April, 1974): 6–18.

Mallery, Garrick. "The Indian Systems of Canada and the United States." *The Nation* 25 (September 6, 1877): 147–49.

Mattison, Ray H. "The Military Frontier on the Upper Missouri," *Nebraska History* 37 (1956).

Morton, W. L. "The Battle of the Grand Coteau, 13–14 July 1851," *Manitoba Scientific and Historical Society Papers*, series 3, no. 16 (1961): 37–49.

Pennanen, Gary. "Sitting Bull: Indian Without a Country." *Canadian Historical Review* 51 (June, 1970): 123–40.

Rickey, Don, Jr. "The Battle of Wolf Mountain." *Montana, the Magazine of Western History* 13 (Spring, 1963), 44–54.

Snell, James G. "The Frontier Sweeps Northwest: American Perceptions of the British American Prairie West of the Point of Canadian Expansion (circa 1870)." *The Western Historical Quarterly* 11 (October, 1980).

Stacey, C. P. "The Military Aspect of Canada's Winning of the West." *Canadian Historical Review* 21 (1940): 1–24.

Stanley, George F. G. "Displaced Red Men: The Sioux in Canada," A. L. Getty and Donald B. Smith, eds., *Western Canadian Reserve Indians Since Treaty* 7 (Vancouver, B.C., 1978): 55–81

Wade, F. "Jean Louis Légaré's Story." *Canadian Magazine*, February 1905, 335.

F. Books

Allison, Edwin H. *The Surrender of Sitting Bull.* Dayton, Ohio: Walker Lithograph and Printing Co., 1891.

Brown, Robert C. *Canada's National Policy 1883–1900: A Study in Canadian-American Relations.* Princeton, N.J.: Princeton University Press, 1964.

Finerty, John F. *Warpath and Bivouac.* Norman: University of Oklahoma Press, 1956.

Frazer, Robert W. *Forts of the West.* Norman: University of Oklahoma Press, 1965.

Gluek, Alvin C., Jr. *Minnesota and the Manifest Destiny of the Canadian Northwest.* Toronto: University of Toronto Press, 1965.

Haydon, A.L. *The Riders of the Plains.* London: Andrew Melrose, 1910.

Hyde, George E. *Spotted Tail's Folk: A History of the Brule Sioux.* Norman: University of Oklahoma Press, 1961.

Johnson, Virginia W. *The Unregimented General: A Biography of Nelson A. Miles.* Boston: Houghton-Mifflin, 1962.

Josephy, Alvin. *The Nez Perce Indians and the Opening of the Northwest.* New Haven, Ct.: Yale University Press, 1965.

Lowie, Robert H. *Indians of the Plains.* New York: Greenwood, 1954.

MacEwan, Grant. *Sitting Bull: The Years in Canada.* Edmonton, Alberta: Hurtig Publishers, 1973.

MacLeod, R. G. *The North-West Mounted Police and Law Enforcement, 1872–1905.* Toronto: University of Toronto Press, 1976.

McWhorter, Lucillius. *Hear Me, My Chiefs!* Caldwell, Id.: Caxton, 1952.

Miles, Nelson A. *Personal Recollections of General Nelson A. Miles.* Chicago: Werner, 1896.

———. *Serving the Republic.* New York: Harper and Brothers, 1911.

Oppenheim, L. *International Law: A Treatise.* Edited by H. Lauterpacht. Vol. 2. London: Longman, Green and Co., 1955.

Nurge, E. *The Modern Sioux, Social Systems and Reservation Culture.* Lincoln, Neb.: University of Nebraska Press, 1970.

Owram, Doug. *Promise of Eden: The Canadian Expansionist Movement and the Idea of the West, 1856–1900.* Toronto: University of Toronto, 1980.

Percy, Algernon Heber. *Journal of Two Excursions in the British North West Territory of North America.* Shropshire, England: Bennion and Horne, 1879.

Prucha, Francis P., ed. *Documents of United States Indian Policy*. Lincoln, Neb.: University of Nebraska Press, 1975.

Sharp, Paul F. *Whoop-up Country*. St. Paul: University of Minnesota Press, 1955.

Thomas, Lewis H. *The Struggle for Responsible Government in the North-West Territories, 1870–1897*. 2d ed. Toronto, 1978.

Turner, C. Frank. *Across the Medicine Line: The Epic Confrontation between Sitting Bull and the North-West Mounted Police*. Toronto: McClelland and Stewart, 1973.

Turner, John Peter. *The North-West Mounted Police*. 2 vols. Ottawa: King's Printer, 1950.

Utley, Robert M. *The Contribution of the Frontier to the American Military Tradition*. Colorado Springs, Colo.: United States Air Force Academy, 1977.

———. *Frontier Regulars: The United States Army on the Frontier, 1866–1891*. New York: MacMillan, 1973.

Vestal, Stanley. *Sitting Bull, Champion of the Sioux: A Biography*. Boston: Houghton-Mifflin, 1932.

Walker, Judson Elliott. *Campaigns of General Custer in the North-West and the Final Surrender of Sitting Bull*. New York: Argonaut Press Reprint, 1966 ed.

Weigley, Russell F. *The American Way of War: A History of United States Military Strategy and Policy*. Bloomington, Ind.: Indiana University Press, 1973.

INDEX